VIKING SOCIETY FOR NORTHERN RESEARCH
TEXT SERIES

GENERAL EDITORS

Anthony Faulkes and Richard Perkins

VOLUME XIII

A HISTORY OF NORWAY

AND

THE PASSION AND MIRACLES OF THE BLESSED ÓLÁFR

A HISTORY OF NORWAY
AND
THE PASSION AND MIRACLES
OF THE BLESSED ÓLÁFR

TRANSLATED BY
DEVRA KUNIN

EDITED WITH AN INTRODUCTION AND NOTES BY
CARL PHELPSTEAD

VIKING SOCIETY FOR NORTHERN RESEARCH
UNIVERSITY COLLEGE LONDON
2001

Printed by Short Run Press Limited, Exeter

ISBN 978 0 903521 48 2

Reprinted with corrections and supplementary note copyright 2017

The cover illustration is based on a wall-painting depicting
St Óláfr on a voyage, illustrating a late medieval legend of a sailing
contest between St Óláfr and his half-brother Haraldr for the
Norwegian crown (see articles in Svahnström 1981, 135–60).
Church at Vallensbæk, Sjælland.

CONTENTS

PREFACE

The introduction and notes to these translations of *Historia Norwegiae* and *Passio et miracula beati Olavi* have been compiled with the needs of students primarily in mind and are designed to provide essential background information and to stimulate further reading of texts listed in the Bibliography.

Complete consistency with regard to the treatment of personal names and place-names in the translations has proved neither possible nor desirable. In general, the aim has been to use the forms most likely to be encountered when reading other texts from or about medieval Scandinavia. Almost all personal names are therefore in their standard Old Norse forms; the exceptions include some Anglo-Saxons, a Russian, biblical names and a few unidentified individuals left in Latin. Place-names in Scandinavia are also usually given in Old Norse where possible, with modern equivalents given in the index of place-names. With one or two exceptions, non-Scandinavian place-names (and all countries) are in their usual English forms.

The Bibliography includes details of the texts to which references are made in abbreviated form. Biblical references are to the Latin Vulgate translation, with parenthetical references to the Authorised Version where this differs.

ACKNOWLEDGEMENTS

Devra Kunin's translations were read by Peter Foote, Joan Turville-Petre and Þorbjörg Helgadóttir before I was invited to introduce and annotate them. Christine Butler and Sarah Newton (respectively Assistant Archivist and Librarian at Corpus Christi College, Oxford) kindly allowed me access to items in their care, including the manuscript of *Passio et miracula beati Olavi*. I am pleased to record my thanks to friends and colleagues who have helped me during my work on these texts, especially Jeremy Brown, Siân Duke, Peter Foote, Sally Mapstone, Andrew Nash, Heather O'Donoghue, Morag Reavley, Gunnhild Røthe and Shaun Tougher. I also owe a debt of gratitude to my parents for their support, and to Mr J. C. S. Scott, thanks to whom I was able to learn Latin at a school which did not normally offer the subject. Above all, I am deeply grateful to Anthony Faulkes and Richard Perkins, the General Editors of the Viking Society Text Series, whose invaluable scrutiny of my work has saved me from sundry errors and infelicities. Any that remain are entirely my own responsibility.

Carl Phelpstead
Cardiff
Feast of St Oswald 2000

SUPPLEMENTARY NOTE (2008)

Publication on the web has provided an opportunity to make a few corrections. In addition, it may be noted that the Dalhousie manuscript that includes *Historia Norwegiae* has now been acquired by the National Archives of Scotland, Edinburgh (MS GD 45/31/1). An important new edition of the Latin text of *Historia Norwegiae* with facing English translation and extensive introduction and commentary is essential reading: *Historia Norwegie*, ed. Inger Ekrem and Lars Boje Mortensen, trans. Peter Fisher (2003); see my review in *Saga-Book* XXVIII (2003), 105–08. Work on *Passio Olavi* since 2001 includes: Lars Boje Mortensen, 'Recent Research in the Legend of Saint Olav' in *Scripturus vitam: lateinische Biographie von der Antike bis in die Gengenwart: Festgabe für Walter Berschin zum 65. Geburtstag*, ed. Dorothea Walz (2002), 1011–18; Lars Boje Mortensen and Else Mundal, 'Erkebispesetet i Nidaros – arnestad og verkstad for Olavslitteraturen' in *Ecclesia Nidrosiensis 1153–1537: søkelys på Nidaroskirkens og Nidarosprovinsens historie,* ed. Steinar Imsen (2003), 353–84. Readers of *Passio Olavi* will also want to consult Martin Chase, ed., *Einar Skúlason's Geisli: A Critical Edition* (2005).

CP

INTRODUCTION

THE TWO WORKS translated in this volume are among the earliest surviving texts from medieval Norway. In addition to their intrinsic value as historical documents providing insights into the period of their composition and the more remote past, they also occupy an important place in the literary history of medieval Norway and Iceland. The purpose of this introduction is to elucidate the literary-historical context of the texts and to provide the reader with some orientation in the exceptionally complex scholarly debate which has surrounded them.

Historia Norwegiae

Historia Norwegiae[1] begins, after a brief Prologue, with a description of Norway and Greenland, a discussion of Lappish customs and descriptions of Orkney and the Hebrides, the Faroes, and Iceland. The rest of the surviving text provides an account of Norwegian history from the legendary beginnings of the Ynglingar dynasty to the return to Norway from England of the future king and martyr, Óláfr Haraldsson, in AD 1015. Markedly disproportionate attention is given in this history to Norway's two missionary kings, Óláfr Tryggvason and Óláfr Haraldsson.

The state of our knowledge about the origins of *Historia Norwegiae* may be summed up in words from a recent article by Inger Ekrem (1998b, 65):

> The medieval text *Historia Norwegie* has been subjected to thorough and frequent scrutiny since its first publication in 1850. Nevertheless it remains to be established when, why, where, for whom and by whom it was written.

The only surviving manuscript of *Historia Norwegiae* (in which it is entitled *Ystoria Norwegie*) is in the private possession of the Earl of Dalhousie at Brechin Castle in Scotland and is consequently known as the Dalhousie manuscript (it is also occasionally referred to as the Panmure Codex, from the former name of the Dalhousie family). This paper manuscript, now comprising 35 leaves, contains

---

[1] Various spellings of the title of this work will be encountered in the scholarship devoted to it.

eight historical texts, seven in Latin and one in Scots English, the first three about Norway and the Norse earldom of Orkney and the other five about Scottish history (Michael Chesnutt, the latest scholar to have access to the manuscript, provides a full description and study of it (1985)). *Historia Norwegiae,* which is the first item in the manuscript (fols 1r–12r), was first edited by Munch under the title *Breve Chronicon Norvegiæ* (1850, 1–18). The translation in this volume has been made from the later edition by Gustav Storm, who provides both a critical and a diplomatic text (1880, 69–124, 203–24).[2]

Chesnutt has disproved Munch's theory that the manuscript may have been commissioned by the last earl of Orkney, William Sinclair (earl 1434–70), but there does seem to be a link between the Sinclair family and the three texts in the manuscript concerning Norway and Orkney. Moreover, a lost copy of *Historia Norwegiae* is known to have existed in Kirkwall, Orkney, in the first half of the fifteenth century, when it was used by the compiler of a genealogy of the earls of Orkney which follows *Historia Norwegiae* in the Dalhousie manuscript, but which is based on a text of that work slightly different from the one which survives (Chesnutt 1985, 67–68; cf. Storm 1880, xvii and Crawford 1977, 174–76). The spelling of Norse names and the orthography of the Scots text indicate that the Dalhousie scribe was a native speaker of Scots (Chesnutt 1985, 69). The manuscript was dated to between 1443 and 1460 by earlier scholars including Storm (1880, xvii), but Chesnutt dates it to *c.*1500–10 (1985, especially pp. 76, 88). He shows that the scribe is to be identified with the scribe of the Haye manuscript from Roslin (Edinburgh, National Library of Scotland MS T.D. 209) who was also responsible for the first part of Oxford, Bodleian Library, MS Arch. Selden B. 24 (one of the most important Scots literary manuscripts, containing among other treasures the only surviving copy of the *Kingis Quair*). The Selden manuscript was written for the Sinclair family and belonged to a grandson of William Sinclair, while the Haye manuscript was owned by the

---

[2] The preparation of a new collaborative edition of Latin texts from medieval Norway, including both *Historia Norwegiae* and the *Passio et miracula beati Olavi,* is now under way (see 'Norwegian Medieval Latin Literature' 1997).

Roslin lairds who were also descendants of William Sinclair. We can therefore attribute these three manuscripts, Selden, Haye, and Dalhousie, to a scribe employed by the senior branch of the Sinclair family during the reign of James IV of Scotland (Chesnutt 1985, 84–88).[3]

Although the surviving manuscript was copied c.1500–10, the date of composition of *Historia Norwegiae* is certainly earlier. Four fourteenth-century lists of Swedish kings that extend down to the year 1333 seem to borrow from a text of *Historia Norwegiae*, which must therefore have been written before c.1330 (Storm 1880, xviii–xix, with a diplomatic edition of these lists on pp. 225–28; see also Steinnes 1946–48, 7–17). As explained below in the notes to the text, the account of islands which pay tribute to Norway suggests a latest possible date of 1266, since after the Peace of Perth agreed in that year Norway recognised the sovereignty of the Scottish king over the Hebrides. There remains, however, considerable disagreement about how much earlier than that *Historia Norwegiae* was written. This question is closely connected to that of the relationship of *Historia Norwegiae* to other early histories from Norway and Iceland, and it is necessary to consider this issue before returning to the question of dating.

Historia Norwegiae belongs to a group of three medieval Norwegian histories now known as the 'Norwegian synoptics' because they each provide a relatively brief overview of a substantial period of Norwegian history. One of the other two Norwegian synoptics is, like *Historia Norwegiae,* in Latin: the *Historia de antiquitate regum Norwagiensium* was written by Theodoricus monachus c.1180. The other is an anonymous text written c.1190 in the Norse vernacular and known as *Ágrip af Noregskonungasǫgum.*

The earliest histories of the Norwegian kings of which we know are two brief epitomes by Icelandic historians of the first half of the twelfth century. Unfortunately, neither of these texts survives today. Sæmundr Sigfússon (1056–1133) is believed to have been the first Icelandic historian, and the anonymous poem *Nóregs konungatal*

---

[3] All three manuscripts were probably copied during the period 1490–1510. The Haye and Selden manuscripts have been attributed to a priest and notary public associated with the Sinclair family called James Graye, but Chesnutt casts doubt on this identification of the scribe (1985, 86–87).

(*c.*1190) claims to follow his account of the Norwegian kings between Haraldr hárfagri and Magnús góði. Sæmundr almost certainly wrote his probably very brief lost history in Latin and Iceland's earliest vernacular historian is Ari Þorgilsson (1067/8–1148). The Preface to his surviving *Íslendingabók* seems to state that it is a revision of an earlier version which included additional genealogical information together with biographies of Norwegian kings (*konunga ævi*; *Íslendingabók* 3). It is uncertain how much information was included in these biographies; they are likely to have been relatively brief, but may nevertheless be the foundations upon which later historical writing in both Iceland and Norway was built.[4]

After Ari, Icelandic historians turned to the composition of biographies of individual Norwegian kings, beginning *c.*1150 with Eiríkr Oddsson's now lost *Hryggjarstykki*, which concentrated on the life of the pretender Sigurðr slembir (d. 1139; see Bjarni Guðnason 1978). This was followed by biographies of the two kings most closely involved in the conversion of Norway to Christianity, Óláfr Tryggvason (r. 995–1000) and St Óláfr Haraldsson (r. 1015–30). Two Latin Lives of Óláfr Tryggvason were written by monks from Þingeyrar: Oddr Snorrason's Life dates from *c.*1190, or maybe earlier, *c.*1170, but survives only in three texts of an Icelandic translation originally made *c.*1200, while our knowledge of Gunnlaugr Leifsson's version of *c.*1200 is limited to what can be deduced about it from later Icelandic sagas which seem to have used it as a source. The sagas of St Óláfr Haraldsson are discussed below in relation to the *Passio et miracula beati Olavi*; the account of the early part of the saint's life in *Historia Norwegiae* may be compared especially with the account in the *Legendary Saga of St Óláfr*, which is now generally thought to reflect closely the contents of the mostly lost *Oldest Saga of St Óláfr* (see further below).

A synthesis of these two approaches to historical writing, that of the brief epitomes of Norwegian history (Ari's lost *konunga ævi* and the Norwegian synoptics) and that of the Icelandic biographies of individual kings, gave rise to vernacular Icelandic Kings' Sagas which cover the reigns of several kings. The earliest of these

---

[4] The possible connections between the Norwegian synoptics and the works of Sæmundr and Ari are briefly discussed below, pp. xiv–xvi.

compendia is *Morkinskinna* (probably compiled *c.*1220; = *Msk*)
but this deals with events between 1030 and 1157 (originally
1177), which is later than the period covered by *Historia Norwegiae*
in its surviving form. The most important Kings' Sagas of the
compendium type for comparison with *Historia Norwegiae* are
therefore later works, especially the anonymous *Fagrskinna* (*c.*1225,
probably written in Norway by either an Icelander or a Norwegian;
= *Fsk*) and Snorri Sturluson's great masterpiece, *Heimskringla*
(*c.*1225–35; = *Hkr*).

Some of the early Norwegian and Icelandic histories are written in Latin and others in Old Norse, but this should not be allowed
to obscure the essential unity of the historiographical tradition,
for Icelandic historians writing in the vernacular were nevertheless deeply influenced by the Latin culture of Europe. Historical
writing in Scandinavia and Iceland during the late twelfth and
thirteenth centuries reflects the increased interest in history and
historical writing which is characteristic of the so-called 'twelfth-
century renaissance'.[5] In particular, medieval Scandinavian and
Icelandic historical writing in both Latin and Old Norse is indebted
to the *Gesta Hammaburgensis ecclesiae pontificum* written by
Adam of Bremen *c.*1068–75 (= *Gesta Hamm.*); Birgit and Peter
Sawyer write that 'The remarkable interest in Scandinavian history
exhibited in the decades after 1170 was not directly caused by
Adam, but none of the historians who wrote then, nor their successors, could escape his influence' (1992, 48). Among those most
deeply influenced by Adam's work was the author of *Historia
Norwegiae*.

The relationships between the early Norwegian and Icelandic
histories have been the subject of extensive scholarly debate
which has focussed on two related issues: the interrelationships
among the so-called 'Norwegian synoptics' (*Historia Norwegiae,
Theodoricus's Historia de antiquitate regum Norwagiensium* and

<hr/>

[5] Cf. Haskins 1927, especially 224–77. For an introduction to medieval
historical writing in general see Smalley 1974. Scandinavian and Iceland-
ic histories are usefully surveyed in articles under 'Historieskrivning' in
KLNM VI, cols 587–602, and by Andersson (1985) and Sawyer and
Sawyer (1992); see also articles on the individual texts and authors in
KLNM and *MSE*.

Ágrip af Noregskonungasǫgum); and the connections between those three texts and Icelandic historical writing. The course of debate on these complex issues up to the early 1980s is concisely and usefully summarised by Andersson (1985, 201–11; see also Ulset 1983, 16–47), and the reader of the brief account which follows is referred there for more detailed references. It is generally assumed on the basis of similarities between the two texts that the author of *Ágrip* made direct use of Theodoricus's work. In addition, the close correspondences between *Ágrip* and *Historia Norwegiae* (conveniently listed in Ulset 1983, 170–82) are so numerous that 'one must stand in literary debt to the other or, more likely, both derive from a common written source' (Andersson 1985, 201). This common source could be the lost Latin history by Sæmundr Sigfússon, or the **konunga ævi* included in the original version of Ari Þorgilsson's *Íslendingabók*, or an otherwise unknown lost Norwegian history. The most thorough discussions of this problem arrive at different conclusions. Bjarni Aðalbjarnarson argues that both *Ágrip* and *Historia Norwegiae* depend on a lost Norwegian-Latin history (1937, 1–54). Svend Ellehøj, on the other hand, argues that the lost common source is Ari's **konunga ævi* (1965, 198–258). As Andersson says, the difference between these two positions 'does not appear great, but the implications of the difference are far-reaching' (1985, 202). If the lost source is a Norwegian text, rather than Ari's Icelandic history, then 'we are led to believe that there was an independent Norwegian school of history writing and that the synoptics are a specifically Norwegian manifestation' (Andersson 1985, 202). If, on the other hand, *Ágrip* and *Historia Norwegiae* depend on Ari's work this, together with Theodoricus's admission of his debt to Icelandic sources (ch. 1), means that medieval Norwegian historical writing was modelled on and indebted to that of Iceland.

Andersson (1985, 203–09) offers a critique of Ellehøj's arguments in favour of Ari's **konunga ævi* being the lost source, clearly demonstrating the shakily hypothetical foundations of his account of the intertextual relations. Andersson concludes that Ellehøj's 'arguments in favour of Ari's **konunga ævi* as a source for the *Historia Norwegiae* lead to an impasse' (1985, 209). While Ellehøj's view could be correct, his evidence is not conclusive and other explanations are also possible. Further alternatives make the situation appear still more complicated. Tor Ulset, for example, argues on stylistic grounds that the author of *Ágrip* translates from both Theodoricus and *Historia Norwegiae* (1983, 64–151) and this does away with the need for a lost common source to explain the correspondences between *Ágrip* and *Historia Norwegiae*. Bjarni Guðnason (1977), on the other hand, argues cogently that Theodoricus made use of Sæmundr and Ari, and Andersson (1985, 210) points out that this argument may logically be extended to explain similarities between the three Norwegian synoptics purely on the basis of their common dependence on Sæmundr and/or Ari. This in turn leads him to suggest that 'such a hypothesis leaves standing very little of the painstaking edifice erected by Bjarni Aðalbjarnarson and Svend Ellehøj, and the question arises whether any cogent analysis of the textual relationships is possible' (1985, 211). Just such a conclusion was anticipated in Siegfried Beyschlag's attempt to deny literary relations between the Norwegian synoptics and argue instead that the close correspondences between them arose as a result of their common debt to *oral* traditions (Beyschlag 1950). This approach has not been favoured by other scholars, but is by its nature impossible to refute definitively.

It is no wonder, then, that Andersson (1985, 211) ends his account of scholarship on the Norwegian synoptics with this sobering conclusion:

> If Beyschlag's theory is rejected and the analyses by Bjarni Aðalbjarnarson and Ellehøj founder on their own disagreement as well as the altered presuppositions suggested by Bjarni Guðnason, we are obliged to conclude that the last fifty years of kings' saga research have left us empty-handed.

The most important intervention in this debate since the publication of Andersson's article is that made by Gudrun Lange (1989). She examines the relationship of *Historia Norwegiae* to a large number of possible Icelandic sources including skaldic verse, the works of Sæmundr and Ari, the *Oldest Saga of St Óláfr* and Oddr Snorrason's Life of Óláfr Tryggvason (Lange 1989, 141–63). She also examines the likely sources for Theodoricus's history and *Ágrip* in a similar way, and this exhaustive study enables her to affirm that, as Andersson (1985, 210) had suggested, all three

Norwegian synoptics *could* have used Sæmundr and Ari. Moreover, she argues that they *could* all also have used skaldic poetry,
the *Oldest Saga of St Óláfr,* and Oddr Snorrason's Latin Life of
Óláfr Tryggvason (1989, 178). She is able, however, to demonstrate only the possibility of such indebtedness, and has to admit
that many different possibilities exist (1989, 178). Despite this, she
concludes that medieval Norwegian historiography was clearly
dependent on that of Iceland, and offers as her solution of what we
might call the 'Norwegian synoptic problem' the observation that
the synoptics may be indirectly related to each other through being
based on common Icelandic sources (1989, 181).

A recently published monograph on *Historia Norwegiae* by Inger
Ekrem explores the possible connections between its composition
and the establishment of a Norwegian archiepiscopal see at Niðaróss
(modern Trondheim) in 1152/3 (on the establishment of the
archbishopric see Helle 1964, 27–31; Gunnes 1996, 50–73). In the
course of her investigation Ekrem offers new arguments about the
date and authorship of *Historia Norwegiae* which, if accepted,
have significant implications for the question of the work's relationship to other Scandinavian and Icelandic histories. We may
therefore return at this point to the question of the date of *Historia
Norwegiae.* A glance at the table of 'results of research 1850–
1989' provided by Ekrem (1998a, 88; also in 1998b, 50) indicates
that datings of the composition of the text have ranged from as
early as the 1150s to as late as *c.*1300, with the majority of scholars
in favour of dates between 1170 and 1220.[6]

Many have been convinced by S. Bugge's comparison of the
text's account of a recent volcanic eruption (10/32–11/4 below)
with a reference to such an event in the Icelandic annals for 1211,
suggesting a date of composition perhaps *c.*1220–30 (Bugge 1873,
35–37; cf. Finnur Jónsson 1928, 275). Storm (1873, 377–78),

---

[6] A sample will make clear both the range of suggested datings and the
lack of scholarly agreement: 1152–63 (Hanssen 1949, 28); *c.*1170 (Koht
1919–20, 102; Schreiner 1927, 73; Ellehøj 1965, 144–46; 295); 1180–90
(Storm 1880, xxiii); 1200–20 (Finnur Jónsson 1920–24, II 596–97; 1928,
276–77; Bjarni Aðalbjarnarson 1937, 20–22); 1260/64–66 (Meissner 1902,
39–43); Maurer (1867, 700–01; 1875, 9) suggests a date not before 1266
but possibly as late as the fifteenth century.

however, asserts the impossibility of being certain that the eruption referred to in the text is the one which took place in 1211, and Koht (1919–20, 104) notes that some versions of the Icelandic annals refer to this event as an earthquake and that similar earthquakes are also recorded in 1164 and 1182. In her discussion of the origins of *Historia Norwegiae* Ekrem argues in favour of an early date of composition, pointing out that none of the certain sources for *Historia Norwegiae* dates from later than *c.*1140 and that its list of rulers of Normandy (p. 9 below) ends with Henry I of England (r. 1100–35), making no mention of Stephen or Henry II. Ekrem argues that the work is therefore likely to have been written between 1140 and 1152–54, perhaps around 1150 (Ekrem 1998a, 8–13). This would make *Historia Norwegiae* the earliest Norwegian national history (Ekrem 1998a, 87; cf. Koht 1919–20) and so would fit best with a view of the relationships between the Norwegian synoptics which explains the agreement between *Ágrip* and *Historia Norwegiae* by positing Sæmundr or Ari rather than a lost Norwegian-Latin synoptic as their common source. Ekrem's dating allows her to associate the composition of *Historia Norwegiae* with the establishment of the archiepiscopal see at Niðaróss in 1152/3 and supports her argument that *Historia Norwegiae* may have been written in order to convince the pope or his legate, Cardinal Nicholas Breakspear, that Norway was worthy of its own archbishopric (1998a, 19; cf. 1998b). If Ekrem's theory is accepted, Breakspear's English nationality might help account for the pro-English bias of *Historia Norwegiae* (cf. Ekrem 1998a, 68, 80–81).[7]

The Prologue to *Historia Norwegiae* implies that after its account of Nordic geography and the history of the kings of Norway down to St Óláfr Haraldsson the work will go on to describe the conversion and Christianisation of Norway (1/11–16 below). That it does not do so confirms that the text which survives is incomplete.

---

[7] A connection with Breakspear's mission might also help to account for the Orcadian connections of the sole surviving manuscript of *Historia Norwegiae*: Ekrem (1998a, 81) speculates that Earl Rǫgnvaldr and Bishop Vilhjálmr of Orkney could have brought a copy of the work back with them after meeting Cardinal Breakspear during the visit they made to Norway *c.*1153.

This could be because the author died before finishing it, or as Ekrem (1998a, 67) suggests, because Nicholas Breakspear's mission to Norway and establishment of the archiepiscopal see made the completion of the book unnecessary. Alternatively, it may be because the interests of those who brought the text to Orkney, or of a later copyist there, were primarily in the Orcadian material contained in what survives of *Historia Norwegiae* rather than in the ecclesiastical history contained in its now lost continuation (cf. Ekrem 1998a, 81).

Whatever the explanation for the now incomplete state of *Historia Norwegiae*, a second 'book' containing an account of the life, death and miracles of St Óláfr Haraldsson would have provided an ideal climax to the complete work and would have fulfilled the stated intentions of the Prologue (cf. Ekrem 1998a, 68).[8] Such a Life might have existed separately before incorporation into *Historia Norwegiae* and might subsequently have taken on an independent existence in ecclesiastical and liturgical use. Ekrem (1998a, 68) suggests that the *Passio et miracula beati Olavi* (discussed and translated below) may be just such an adaptation of what was originally Book II of *Historia Norwegiae*, provided now with its own introduction including some of the geographical and historical material found earlier in *Historia Norwegiae*. The fact that St Óláfr's chief opponent in both *Historia Norwegiae* and the *Passio Olavi* is Knútr Sveinsson of Denmark, whereas in the Norwegian Homily Book version of the Life of Óláfr (discussed below) it is the Norwegian chieftain Kálfr Árnason, is a significant point of contact between the two texts, one which Ekrem suggests reflects the anti-Danish/pro-English bias in *Historia Norwegiae* and in certain miracles in the *Passio et miracula beati Olavi* (1998a, 85–86).[9]

---

[8] Note, however, that Ulset (1983, 147–48) suggests the work may originally have continued to at least the year 1155, and Storm (1880, xxviii) believes it could have gone up to the author's own time (the late twelfth century, in Storm's opinion). Schreiner (1927, 84), on the other hand, claims that the text would not have continued past St Óláfr's death at the Battle of Stiklarstaðir.

[9] This anti-Danish bias may reflect the fact that until the foundation of the archbishopric of Niðaróss the Norwegian church was subject to the archiepiscopal see of Lundr in the Danish kingdom.

The question of the authorship of *Historia Norwegiae* is necessarily bound up with that of the identity of the Agnellus to whom the work is dedicated (see 1/27 and corresponding note below). Munch (1850, ii, vi) argued in favour of Orcadian authorship largely on the basis of manuscript provenance and the knowledge of Orkney displayed in the text. Ample evidence that the author must have been Norwegian is, however, provided by phrases such as 'our kings' (10/6), 'which we call Hólmgarðr' (23/23) and 'our Óláfr' (24/34), together with the forms of some of the personal and place-names in the text (on which see Storm 1880, xix; Hægstad 1919–20; Skard 1930, 12–15).[10] Bugge argued that the text was written by a Norwegian in Orkney (1873, 37–41), but there is somewhat more convincing evidence that the Norwegian author may have written either while living in Denmark or after returning to Norway from there. In particular, it seems the author of *Historia Norwegiae* used a particular manuscript in Denmark which contained copies of texts by Adam of Bremen, Honorius Augustodunensis and possibly Solinus which he used as sources. This manuscript, known as the Sorø codex, was destroyed in the fire in the Royal Library, Copenhagen in 1728 (see Steinnes 1946–48, 17–32; cf. Ellehøj 1965, 146–47; further arguments in favour of a connection with Denmark are put forward by Sandaaker (1985)). The author must certainly have studied abroad, probably in France (Koht 1919–20, 113–17; though cf. Skard 1930, 85), but possibly in England (Storm 1880, xxiii). He seems to have written with a non-Norwegian audience in mind, as is evident from the opening description of Norway, the translation of Norse nicknames into Latin, and the proposed identifications of Agnellus, the work's dedicatee, with Englishmen of that name (see note to 1/27).

Attempts have been made to identify the anonymous Norwegian author of *Historia Norwegiae* with known individuals, but no candidate has won much support and such attempts at identification necessarily rest on very shaky foundations given our uncertainty about the date of the text's composition and our lack of

---

[10] Finnur Jónsson (1920–24, II 598–99) and Paul Lehmann (1936–37, 2:75) nevertheless thought the author must have been an English or German cleric living in Norway.

biographical information from the period.[11] After surveying earlier scholarly opinion, Ekrem argues that *Historia Norwegiae* could well be an early work of the future Archbishop Eysteinn Erlendsson, to whom the *Passio et miracula beati Olavi* is also attributed (1998a, 71–79; on Eysteinn's authorship of the *Passio Olavi* see further below).[12] Ekrem compares Eiliv Skard's stylistic studies of *Historia Norwegiae* (1930) and the *Passio et miracula beati Olavi* (1932) and suggests that such differences of style as there are between the two texts are not incompatible with their being the work of a single author, one who could have written *Historia Norwegiae* relatively early in his career and then later in life adapted what was originally the second book of that text to produce a self-sufficient account of the passion and miracles of St Óláfr.

In her recent work on *Historia Norwegiae* Ekrem (1998a; 1998b) makes a strong case for seeing it as propaganda for the establishment of an archiepiscopal see at Niðaróss. In the conclusion of her monograph she identifies four aims which the author seems to have hoped to further by writing *Historia Norwegiae* (Ekrem 1998a, 79; more detailed reference to her arguments will be found in the notes to the text below). These aims are: the establishment of a national ecclesiastical province based at Niðaróss (hence the anti-Danish and pro-English bias of the text); the inclusion within that province of all lands which pay tribute to Norway or which were Christianised from Norway (the lands described at the beginning of *Historia Norwegiae* are precisely those incorporated into the archdiocese); the establishment of a new episcopal see in the Uppland region (hence the emphasis on that region in the text; a new bishopric was founded at Hamar at the same time as the archdiocese was created);

[11] Attempts at such identification include Koht 1919–20, 109–17, Steinnes 1946–48, 32–59 and Steinnes 1965, 27–43.

[12] Ekrem also, less enthusiastically, offers an alternative explanation according to which Eysteinn may be the dedicatee of the work, which may then have been written by the Rǫgnvaldr who was later consecrated bishop of the Hebrides and Isle of Man, perhaps by Cardinal Breakspear in Norway in 1153 (1998a, 80; cf. 17, 78). Ekrem even briefly considers the possibility that Eysteinn might be both author and dedicatee of the work, something she claims might be understandable in a medieval context in which fictional dedicatees often appear in prefaces and prologues (1998a, 78–79).

and the canonisation of Óláfr Tryggvason (accounting for the disproportionate attention given to his life and the many parallels between it and the life of Norway's accepted royal saint, Óláfr Haraldsson). Ekrem suggests that the text was written before 1152/3 to further these four aims (all but the last of which were in fact achieved). Although her account of the origins of *Historia Norwegiae* is cogent and in many ways attractive, it is also at times highly speculative; rather than providing a definitive solution to the problems of the date, authorship and purpose of *Historia Norwegiae,* she offers yet another set of possibilities. Proponents of a later date for the text might accept her analysis of its ideological position yet argue that it was written after the establishment of the archdiocese in order retrospectively to justify the new situation. Ekrem has pushed back the earliest possible date of the text to *c.*1150, but without conclusively rebutting the arguments of those who favour a date in the later twelfth or early thirteenth century. Much, of course, depends on the view taken of the relationship of *Historia Norwegiae* to other early Norwegian and Icelandic historical writing, but here there is unfortunately always a danger of circularity since neither the date of the text nor its relationship to other texts is certain. A belief that *Historia Norwegiae* depends upon some earlier text presupposes a later dating, whereas a belief in an earlier date rules out the possibility of its being dependent on the other text.

References to the most important parallels and possible sources for material in *Historia Norwegiae* will be found in the notes below, but it will perhaps also be useful briefly to list those whose relationship to *Historia Norwegiae* has not yet been discussed here, while noting that in some cases there is little certainty as to whether or not the writer of *Historia Norwegiae* did actually know the text in question. Although there is no mention of Adam of Bremen in *Historia Norwegiae* it is clear that his *Gesta Hammaburgensis ecclesiae pontificum* was one of the most important models for the Norwegian historian. The two texts contain a similar mix of geographical, historical and church historical material, and *Historia Norwegiae* may also be seen as a response to Adam's ideological objectives. Whereas Adam emphasised the role of Hamburg–Bremen in the Christianisation of Scandinavia in an attempt to maintain that archbishopric's hold on its northern dioceses,

Historia Norwegiae implicitly supports Norwegian ecclesiastical independence and emphasises the English rather than German involvement in the conversion of Norway. Echoes of Adam's work are most clearly visible in *Historia Norwegiae* in its Prologue, the geographical descriptions and the account of St Óláfr. With the exception of allusions to Virgil's *Aeneid*, which the author seems to have known at first hand, such echoes as there are of classical Latin texts in *Historia Norwegiae* can be attributed to the author's acquaintance with one or more *florilegia*, anthologies of classical quotations popular in the Middle Ages (cf. Skard 1930, 68–72). The author did, however, use the medieval Latin *Imago mundi* (also known as *De imagine mundi*) by Honorius Augustodunensis (*c*.1110). There are clear traces of this in *Historia Norwegiae* (see Skard 1930, 78–83; Steinnes 1946–48, 18–29) but no specific reference to Honorius or his work. There is, on the other hand, a reference to Solinus (11/8 below), the author of a work known variously as *Collectanea rerum mirabilium, De mirabilibus mundi* or *Polyhistor* (*c*.200), though there is no other evidence of the author's use of his text. Honorius, however, did use Solinus's work, and manuscript *scholia* in the Sorø codex drawing attention to this might have misled the author of *Historia Norwegiae* into thinking that Solinus was the author of *Imago mundi,* or that it was substantially based on his work. Alternatively, the reference to Solinus may be intended to indicate that *Historia Norwegiae* is conceived as a supplement to Solinus's work, telling of similar marvels but in the northern areas of Europe which Solinus neglected (Ekrem 1998a, 24–25). The reference to Solinus (who, incidentally, is cited more than once by Adam of Bremen) may even be a deliberate deception; it was not uncommon for medieval writers to disguise their debt to a contemporary source by citing an antique one (Skard 1930, 81).

It has generally been agreed that information on Norman dukes and English kings in *Historia Norwegiae* is derived from the *Descriptio genealogiae ducum Normannorum* in a short English chronicle composed during the reign of Henry II, the *Liber de legibus Angliae.* This is now found (in probably abbreviated form) in manuscripts of the Chronicle of Roger of Howden (ed. Stubbs 1868–71, II 215–52; see Storm 1880, xxi–xxii). Ellehøj (1965, 161–74), however, argues that the information on Norman dukes in *Historia Norwegiae* is so similar to that found in other Norse texts as to suggest that they all derive this information from Ari's lost *konunga ævi*, which the Prologue to Snorri Sturluson's *Heimskringla* says included information about kings in England (*Hkr* I 6). If this were the case, and it is by no means certain, any connection between *Historia Norwegiae* and Anglo-Norman historiography would be via Ari's work.

The close similarities between the description of the habits of beavers in the section of *Historia Norwegiae* dealing with the Lapps and similar descriptions in the works of Gerald of Wales have often been remarked on and it seems likely that the two writers depend upon a common source (see further the note to 5/28 below). A reference to the Prophecies of Merlin (9/25) suggests an acquaintance with Geoffrey of Monmouth's *Historia regum Britanniae* or more probably with an intermediate text, possibly the Chronicle of Orderic Vitalis (see Skard 1930, 76–77 and the note to 9/25–26 below).

Lange argues that it is possible, though no more certain than that, that the author of *Historia Norwegiae* made use of a number of Norse sources. In addition to Ari, these include several skaldic poems: Hallfreðr vandræðaskáld's *Óláfsdrápa*, Halldórr ókristni's *Eiríksflokkr*, Óttarr svarti's *Hǫfuðlausn*, and Sigvatr Þórðarson's *Víkingarvísur* (Lange 1989, 143–44). Similarities between *Historia Norwegiae* and the *Legendary Saga of St Óláfr* (which is held to represent the contents of the *Oldest Saga of St Óláfr*) suggest that the *Historia Norwegiae* could have drawn on the *Oldest Saga of St Óláfr* (Lange 1989, 156–58). Lange also notes many points of agreement between *Historia Norwegiae* and the Life of Óláfr Tryggvason by Oddr Snorrason, especially in their descriptions of Norway; again it is not impossible, but nor is it certain, that *Historia Norwegiae* is indebted to the Icelander's work (Lange 1989, 158–63).

The floridly rhetorical Latin of *Historia Norwegiae* has won its author few modern admirers. It is described by Munch, for instance, as 'turgidus et inflatus' ('turgid and inflated'; 1850, vi) and by Turville-Petre as 'not pleasing' (1967, 175). It may perhaps be thought of as reflecting youthful exuberance, a conceit which would fit well with Ekrem's suggested attribution of the text to the young

Eysteinn Erlendsson. The Latin Vulgate Bible was one of the most significant influences on the language and style of *Historia Norwegiae* (Skard 1930, 63–68). There are nearly four times as many allusions to the Old Testament as to the New; the Psalms are alluded to more than any other book, but there is also much use of the biblical wisdom literature (especially Ecclesiasticus and Wisdom) and the Books of Maccabees. The author's familiarity with the Bible suggests that he must have had particular theological interests which led him to the books he echoes most frequently. He demonstrates a much better knowledge of the Bible than would be expected of an ordinary priest or than is displayed by Theodoricus, who was a monk (Skard 1930, 67–68).

Many rhetorical figures are employed in *Historia Norwegiae*. These include metonymy, periphrasis, litotes, *apo koinou* constructions, parallelism, much use of *figura etymologica*, hyperbaton, much alliteration, and some rhyme (Skard 1930, 52–62). The author shows a particular fondness for synonyms (Skard 1930, 23) and for *variatio sermonis*, the avoidance of the same words in quick succession (Skard 1930, 40–41, 49–52). For more detailed treatment of the style of *Historia Norwegiae* than is appropriate in this introduction to an English translation the reader should consult Skard (1930) and Ulset (1983).

Comparison of the content of *Historia Norwegiae* with other sources for the early history of Norway and its neighbours reveals many points of agreement as well as some differences. It is unfortunately not always possible now to verify (or disprove) information given in these early sources or to decide between alternative accounts. The agreement of several sources cannot necessarily be taken as indicative of historical reliability since their intertextual relationships often mean they are not independent witnesses. On the other hand, uncorroborated material found in only one surviving text is not necessarily incorrect and, as the notes below indicate, the accuracy of information found in no medieval texts other than *Historia Norwegiae* is sometimes confirmed by much later sources.

The considerable difference between the approaches of medieval and modern historians to their task is well illustrated by the fact that not a single date is given for events in *Historia Norwegiae*. Moreover, to the modern reader *Historia Norwegiae* appears to mix historical and geographical fact with legend and pure fiction. It may be helpful to remember that medieval historians, like some postmodernist theorists, viewed historical writing as a rhetorical enterprise which fittingly drew on the imagination in order to express most persuasively what was perceived to be historical truth. As Hayden White (1978, 123) writes,

> prior to the French Revolution, historiography was conventionally regarded as a literary art. More specifically, it was regarded as a branch of rhetoric and its 'fictive' nature generally recognised.

Such an understanding of the nature of medieval historical writing highlights its importance and great value as source material for understanding the beliefs and *mentalité* of the period of its composition, however unreliable it may be as a narrative of earlier events. Ekrem's recent analysis (1998a and 1998b) of the ideological aims of *Historia Norwegiae* demonstrates how stimulating such an approach to historical writing of the past can be.

Passio et miracula beati Olavi

After a career as a viking in northern and western Europe, Óláfr Haraldsson won the kingdom of Norway from Earl Sveinn Hákonarson at the Battle of Nesjar in 1016.[13] As king, Óláfr acquired a reputation for strict but unbiased justice and continued the conversion of Norway to Christianity initiated by his namesake, Óláfr Tryggvason. Óláfr's rule became unpopular and in 1029 Knútr ríki Sveinsson (Canute the Great) of Denmark and England took advantage of a Norwegian uprising against Óláfr to establish his own control over Norway. Óláfr fled to Russia, but returned the following year in an attempt to win back his kingdom. This failed when Óláfr was killed at the Battle of Stiklarstaðir (modern Stiklestad) on 29 July 1030.[14]

Miracles were reported soon after Óláfr's death, and disaffection with Danish rule under Knútr's son, Sveinn, fostered belief in

[13] On Óláfr's life, see e.g. Jones 1984, 374–86; *ODS* 375–76; Reidar Astås, 'Óláfr, St.' in *MSE* 445–46. Articles in Svahnström 1981 address various aspects of Óláfr's life and cult.

[14] On the Battle of Stiklarstaðir see Jón Viðar Sigurðsson, 'Stiklestad, Battle of' in *MSE* 610–11; on the date of Óláfr's death see the note to 31/21–23 below.

Óláfr's sanctity. Just over a year after his death, on 3 August 1031, Óláfr's body was exhumed and then enshrined in Christ Church in Niðaróss. His shrine became the centre of a cult and later, in 1152/3, the seat of an archdiocese which covered Iceland, Greenland, the Faroes, Orkney and Shetland, the Hebrides and the Isle of Man, as well as Norway. Following Knútr's death in 1035 Óláfr's son Magnús returned from exile in Russia to become king. During his reign the cult of his father became firmly established in Norway and spread rapidly elsewhere. Óláfr became the most popular and the most widely venerated Scandinavian saint.

The speed with which Óláfr's cult spread beyond Norway is evident from the appearance of the earliest liturgy for his feast day in England only about twenty years after his death.[15] Writing in the 1070s Adam of Bremen states that Óláfr's feast is celebrated by all the peoples bordering the Baltic (*Gesta Hamm.* II.lxi (59)). Churches were dedicated to Óláfr in England, Scotland, Ireland, the Isle of Man and probably Sweden and Byzantium (cf. Dickins 1937–45; *ODS* 376). St Óláfr also became one of the most popular saints in Iceland (Cormack 1994, 138–44).

The *Passio et miracula beati Olavi* translated here has a complex textual history. Essentially, there are two surviving versions in Latin; certain vernacular texts also provide evidence for the history of the work. The shorter of the two Latin versions is entitled *Acta sancti Olavi regis et martyris* by Storm in his edition in *Monumenta*

---

[15] There is a votive mass for Óláfr's feast day in the Sherborne service book known as the Red Book of Darley (MS Cambridge, Corpus Christi College 422) from the early 1060s (see Warren 1883, 272, 274) and a Latin office for his feast day in the English Leofric Collectar of *c.*1050, MS London, British Library Harley 2961 (ed. Dewick and Frere 1914–21, I, cols 209–14). The office is a compilation of biblical quotations, especially from Ecclesiasticus, which provides almost no historical information about the saint and contains none of the legendary material found in the *Passio Olavi.* On these and other liturgical texts concerning St Óláfr see Gjerløw 1967; 1968, 124–28. The earliest English reference to Óláfr's sanctity is roughly contemporary with the Leofric Collectar: the Abingdon (C) text of the *Anglo-Saxon Chronicle* (I 157) records Óláfr's death in the entry for 1030 (probably written *c.*1050), adding that he 'wæs syððan halig' ('he was afterwards a saint'). On Óláfr's cult in Britain see Dickins 1937–45 and Fell 1981a, 95–96.

historica Norvegiæ (Storm 1880, 125–44). The longer Latin text is called *Passio et miracula beati Olavi* in Metcalfe's edition (1881); it is this version which is translated here, from Metcalfe's text. In what follows I shall use an abbreviation of Storm's title, *Acta Olavi*, when referring specifically to the shorter version and *Passio Olavi* when referring to the longer or to both versions.

The shorter version edited by Storm was widely disseminated in the form of lessons for Óláfr's feast day and is found in a number of manuscript and early printed sources from France, England, Germany and Scandinavia. The oldest surviving text of the *Acta Olavi* came to light after Storm's edition, in 1901 (see 'Catalogus codicum hagiographicorum latinorum bibliothecae publicae Duacensis' 1901, 369–70). This is a *Legendarium* from the Benedictine monastery of Anchin near Arras, MS Douai 295, from *c*.1200 (dated to the last third of the twelfth century in Mortensen 2000a, 96; see now also 2000b). Two chapters on Óláfr from William of Jumièges's *Gesta Normannorum ducum* are appended to the text of the *Acta*. Another text is contained in Oxford, Bodleian Library, MS Rawlinson C440, an early fourteenth-century manuscript from a Cistercian monastery in the diocese of York. A manuscript of *c*.1400, the *Codex Bodecensis*, which belonged to the Augustinian canons in Böddeken in the diocese of Paderborn, is now lost, but was edited by the Bollandists in *Acta sanctorum* (*Julii* VII, 124–27). This edition was then used by Storm as the basis for his text (Storm 1880, 125–44). Two other manuscripts are the Swedish *Liber Laurentii Odonis* of *c*.1400 (Dresden, Sächsische Landesbibliothek MS A182) and a legendary of *c*.1500–12 (the Codex Neoclaustrensis) written by an Augustinian canon of Bordesholm in the diocese of Slesvig (Wiener-Neustadt, Neukloster XII D 21). A number of printed Breviaries from the late fifteenth and early sixteenth centuries also contain passages of the *Acta Olavi* as lessons for Óláfr's feast day (fuller details of the extant texts of the *Acta Olavi* may be found in Storm 1880, xxxi–xxxii; Gjerløw 1967, cols 561–62; 1968, 125–26; liturgical texts are printed in Storm 1880, 229–82; see also Ekrem 2000, with a useful table of the contents of different texts on pp. 112–13). Storm took the vernacular *Old Norwegian Homily Book*, which includes a translation of a lost Latin text of the *Acta Olavi* (see below, pp. xxxiv–xxxv) as a guide to the original form and contents of the *Acta Olavi*, which he reassembled from the *Acta sanctorum* edition and lections in the *Breviarium Nidrosiense* (published Paris 1519) and other early printed breviaries (see Storm 1880, xxxi). The *Acta Olavi* as edited by Storm begins with a brief Life, concentrating on Óláfr's passion. Scholars call this either a *vita* or a *passio*; to avoid confusion with the title *Passio Olavi* for the whole work I shall refer to it as the *vita*, the title used at the end of this section (Metcalfe 1881, 74).[16] The *vita* is followed by a collection of twenty miracle stories, the last of which breaks off very near its beginning. Storm left gaps in his edition for five miracle stories found in the vernacular *Old Norwegian Homily Book* but not in any of the Latin sources known to him (nos XII, XIII, XV, XVI, XVII; 42/7–47/2, 47/18–51/22 in the text translated below).

In 1881 F. Metcalfe published his edition of the *Passio et miracula beati Olaui* from a manuscript discovered after the production of Storm's edition. This is a much longer text; it includes the five miracles for which Storm left gaps in his edition (thus confirming that Storm's reconstruction was essentially correct) and adds around thirty additional miracle stories. The existence of the two different versions immediately raises the question of priority. Metcalfe implies that the *Acta Olavi* was a later abbreviation of the *Passio Olavi*: he states that the *Old Norwegian Homily Book* (whose contents correspond to those of the *Acta Olavi*) was supposed to represent the 'complete work' until discovery of the Corpus Christi manuscript which is 'fuller still' (1881, 49). Sigurður Nordal argues that the longer *Passio Olavi* would have been abbreviated because it was too long for liturgical use (1914, 135). If the text were being abbreviated for liturgical purposes, however, one might expect a selection of miracles to be made from the text as a whole, rather

---

[16] Though a *passio* concentrates on a martyr's death and a *vita* gives more attention to the life of a saint before his or her death, it is often difficult (as here) to make a clear distinction between the two hagiographic genres. The Douai and Bordesholm manuscripts and some early printed breviaries have a shortened version of the *vita* of St Óláfr. Ekrem (2000, 121–28) argues that the shorter *vita* is the original and that this was expanded in a subsequent revision of the text. Østrem (2000, 188–89), on the other hand, attributes the differences between the two *vitae* to their different intended functions: the shorter for liturgical use and the longer as a 'para-liturgical' text for general edificatory reading.

than simply using all of the first twenty or twenty-one miracles; we shall see below that subsequent research has demonstrated that the *Passio Olavi* is in fact a later expansion of the *Acta Olavi.* The longer text printed by Metcalfe is preserved in only one manuscript, which dates from *c.*1200 and belonged to Fountains Abbey, though it is now Corpus Christi College Oxford MS 209. This clearly written and well-preserved manuscript, bound in a sealskin *chemise,* contains five religious works copied by several scribes; the *Passio Olavi* occupies folios 57–90, preceded by two works of St Augustine and followed by two works with particular connections to the Cistercian Fountains Abbey. Mistakes in Scandinavian names in the *Passio Olavi* suggest that its scribe was not of Scandinavian origin, and the manuscript was probably copied in England near the beginning of the thirteenth century (see Metcalfe 1881, 1–2; Mortensen, 2000a, 96, dates the manuscript to the last third of the twelfth century). Fountains Abbey (founded 1132) had a daughter house at Lyse (Lysekloster), twenty miles south of Bergen, which was founded in 1146 (Metcalfe 1881, 2–3; France 1992, 77–85, 522) and interest in Norway's protomartyr at Fountains Abbey may have been stimulated by the connections between these two monasteries.

The (longer) *Passio et miracula beati Olavi* may be divided into four parts. The first two, i. e. the account of Óláfr's life and passion (*vita*) and the first twenty miracles (twenty-one counting the vision before Stiklarstaðir), correspond to and are almost identical to the entire text of the *Acta Olavi* (except that the *Passio* has the Latin text for the five miracle stories missing from the *Acta*).[17] The miracle stories which both versions of the Latin text have in common also appear in vernacular versions including the *Old Norwegian Homily Book* and the *Legendary Saga of St Óláfr* (to be discussed below). The remaining thirty or so miracle stories in the *Passio Olavi* do not appear elsewhere. They divide into two

---

[17] In the *Acta Olavi* and the *Old Norwegian Homily Book* Óláfr's dream before the Battle of Stiklarstaðir is recounted in the *vita* and so not included in the numbering of the miracles in the *miracula* section, hence miracle number twenty in those texts, the healing of a Norwegian king, is the twenty-first miracle if one includes the dream at Stiklarstaðir (which *is* placed in the *miracula* section of the longer *Passio Olavi*).

groups: a continuation apparently updating the first collection (53/6–61/18) is followed by an 'additional treatise' (61/19–74/25) compiled by one 'Bishop Eysteinn' (*Augustinus episcopus*) and including miracles in which he was involved or of which he had heard at first hand.

In 1920 Aarno Malin drew attention to a thirteenth-century manuscript fragment from a Finnish breviary which suggests that there may once have been an even fuller text of the *Passio Olavi* than that edited by Metcalfe from Corpus Christi College Oxford MS 209. The Finnish manuscript contains the *vita* of Óláfr from the *Acta/ Passio Olavi* plus three miracle stories; one of these, involving an English knight (*Miles quidam de Britannia*), is missing from the Latin *Passio Olavi* and from the vernacular *Old Norwegian Homily Book*, although it is in the Douai, Rawlinson, and Bordesholm manuscripts and in later vernacular texts (in the Douai manuscript the story occurs after the story of the mutilated priest (Metcalfe 1881, 82/4 = 39/21 below); Skard (1932, 2) refers to this as the story's correct place). The text in the Douai manuscript and the Helsinki fragment ends with a concluding section which is also found at the end of the miracle stories in the vernacular *Old Norwegian Homily Book*. Malin (1920, 20–27) argues convincingly that rather than being a later interpolation this additional miracle story belonged to the original text.

Storm argued that the author of the *Acta Olavi* must have been a cleric at the cathedral in Niðaróss (1880, xxxv). The discovery of the longer text of the *Passio Olavi* with its ascription of the 'additional treatise' to Bishop Eysteinn led Metcalfe to attribute the hitherto anonymous *Acta/Passio Olavi* to Eysteinn (Øystein) Erlendsson, Archbishop of Niðaróss 1161–88. Eysteinn studied at the school of St Victor in Paris (Bagge 1984, 2–3; Gunnes 1996, 26–49) before becoming a chaplain to the Norwegian king Ingi (r. 1136–61). He was nominated second Archbishop of Niðaróss in 1157, was consecrated by the pope and returned to Norway in 1161. Eysteinn endeavoured to implement the Gregorian reforms in Norway and encouraged clerical celibacy. He supervised the rebuilding of the cathedral in Niðaróss which housed St Óláfr's shrine and was involved in liturgical revision there (Gjerløw 1968, 29–30). He obtained concessions for the church from the secular power when, at Erlingr skakki's request, he crowned Erlingr's eight-year-old son Magnús as king in 1163/4.[18] Between the death of Sigurðr Jórsalafari in 1130 and 1208 Norway was periodically riven by civil war between rival claimants to the throne. Archbishop Eysteinn supported King Magnús Erlingsson against Sverrir Sigurðarson, a pretender claiming descent from King Sigurðr Jórsalafari, and when Sverrir defeated Magnús in 1180 Eysteinn fled to England and excommunicated the new king. In England Eysteinn was supported by Henry II (who had undergone penance for his part in the death of his own archbishop, St Thomas Becket) and stayed at the abbey of Bury St Edmunds from 9 August 1181 to 16 February 1182. Jocelin of Brakelond refers to the archbishop's stay at the abbey in his *Chronicle*, and tells how Eysteinn helped the monks to obtain their choice of abbot from the king (Butler 1949, 15–16). Eysteinn returned to Norway in 1183 and was reconciled with King Sverrir. He then continued the re-building of the cathedral in Niðaróss which housed St Óláfr's shrine. Eysteinn was himself considered a saint immediately after his death on 26 January 1188; his sanctity was confirmed by a local synod in Niðaróss in 1229 and from then until 1268 pleas for his papal canonisation were directed to Rome. A letter from Pope Gregory IX dated 20 April 1241 orders an enquiry into Eysteinn's miracles with a view to his canonisation (*DN* I 18–19). The English monk and historian Matthew Paris, who visited Norway in 1248, refers to posthumous miracles performed by Eysteinn as proof of his sanctity.[19]

Before considering further whether the shorter or longer version of the *Passio Olavi* came first and the extent to which Eysteinn was responsible for either text, it is necessary to mention some other early accounts of St Óláfr's miracles. These provide evidence of early hagiographic traditions about the saint and include parallels to individual miracle stories in the *Passio Olavi*.

[18] Magnús's coronation was the first in Scandinavia. In a charter issued at the coronation or soon after, Magnús committed Norway to the protection of St Óláfr and 'received' the realm from him as a fief. Óláfr figured in the propaganda of both sides in the civil war between Magnús Erlingsson and Sverrir Sigurðarson. On Scandinavian coronations and their links with royal saints' cults, see Hoffmann 1990.

[19] On Eysteinn's life and cult see Metcalfe 1881, 49–57; *ODS* 36 under 'Augustine (Eystein) of Trondheim'; Gunnes (1996).

The earliest evidence for the veneration of St Óláfr is provided
not by ecclesiastical texts in Latin but by skaldic poetry composed
soon after his death. Þórarinn loftunga's *Glælognskviða* ('Sea-
Calm Lay') dates from c.1032.[20] The poem is addressed to King
Sveinn Knútsson and recommends that he ask for the prayers of St
Óláfr. Þórarinn refers to bells which ring of their own accord at
Óláfr's shrine, the uncorrupted state of the saint's body and con-
tinued growth of his hair and nails, and the healing of blind people
at the shrine. Writing in the first half of the thirteenth century,
Snorri Sturluson regarded Þórarinn as an eyewitness source for the
miracles of St Óláfr; he notes that 'Þórarinn loftunga var þá með
Sveini konungi ok sá ok heyrði þessi stórmerki heilagleiks Óláfs
konungs' (*Hkr* II 409; 'Þórarinn loftunga was then with King
Sveinn and saw and heard these great signs of the holiness of King
Óláfr'). Sigvatr Þórðarson's *Erfidrápa* ('Memorial Poem') dates
from c.1040.[21] Sigvatr tells of the same miracles as Þórarinn,
though in a little more detail, and also refers to an eclipse associated with Óláfr's death.[22] Sigvatr also provides evidence that by
the early 1040s mass was already being celebrated in Óláfr's honour in Norway (stanza 25). This in turn suggests that some kind of
account of the saint suitable for recitation at such services must
have existed by that time (cf. Holtsmark 1956, 16). The poems by
Þórarinn and Sigvatr provide important early evidence of Óláfr's
reputation for miracle-working sanctity, but give few actual details.
    An important later skaldic poem on the saint which goes into
some more detail is Einarr Skúlason's *Óláfsdrápa* or *Geisli* ('Sun-
beam'),[23] which he recited at the celebrations marking the establishment of the archiepiscopal see at Niðaróss in 1152/3. Among
the fourteen miracles which Einarr describes are eight of the first
nine miracles (counting the dream before Stiklarstaðir) in the *Passio
Olavi*, a fact which we shall see provides clues about the 'prehistory'
of the Latin text (see the notes for details of these parallels).

[20] *Skjd.* A I 324–27; B I 300–01.
[21] *Skjd.* A I 257–65; B I 239–45.
[22] The eclipse in fact took place a month later, on 31 August 1030
(Liestøl 1932, especially pp. 1–17, 27–28); Sigvatr was in Rome when
Óláfr was martyred and not at Stiklarstaðir.
[23] *Skjd.* A I 459–73; B I 427–45.

A record of Óláfr's miracles would have been kept at his shrine as evidence of his sanctity and to provide edificatory material in support of his cult. The following words from the beginning of the 'additional treatise by Bishop Eysteinn' may refer to written accounts of miracles earlier than the surviving *Passio Olavi* (these may, of course, be identical with the earlier work to which the additional treatise is appended):

> Having read all those accounts which antiquity has entrusted to us concerning the life and miracles of the blessed Óláfr, we deem it fitting that we, who have been personally enlightened by his widespread miracles in our own day, should also commit to the attention of future generations, in writing, those things which have been performed by miraculous powers, to his greater glory, as we have seen for ourselves or have learnt from the testimony of truthful men. (61/21–28 below)

Further evidence of an early collection of miracle stories may be provided by a work dedicated to Archbishop Eysteinn, the *Historia de antiquitate regum Norwagiensium* by Theodoricus monachus. Theodoricus refers to miracles of St Óláfr in Chapter 20 of his work: 'But because all these things have been recorded by several, I regard it as unnecessary to dwell on matters which are already known' (McDougall and McDougall 1998, 33). Scholars usually assume that Theodoricus is here referring to one or more now lost written accounts of Óláfr's translation and miracles (sometimes referred to as *Translatio sancti Olavi*; see McDougall and McDougall 1998, 92 n. 213 for references).

The oldest vernacular prose accounts of Óláfr's miracles to survive are two fragments comprising MS AM 325 IV α 4to, and a collection of miracle stories in the *Old Norwegian Homily Book*. The two leaves of MS AM 325 IV α 4to were published by Storm in 1893 as the final two of the eight fragments in his edition of all that remains of the so-called *Oldest Saga of St Óláfr*. Jonna Louis-Jensen, however, has since re-edited these two leaves and shown that they do not in fact belong with the other fragments (1970). The first leaf of AM 325 IV α 4to probably comes from an otherwise now lost Norse Legendary of St Óláfr (Louis-Jensen 1970, 47; Jónas Kristjánsson 1972, 161). All but the fifth of the six miracle stories contained in this leaf are recounted in the Latin *Passio Olavi* (see the notes to the translation below for details). The leaf appears to be Icelandic and from the mid thirteenth century; a reference to the visit to Norway in 1152/3 of the papal legate Cardinal Nicholas Breakspear (later Pope Hadrian IV) together with the fact that the surviving leaf is clearly a copy of an earlier text led Louis-Jensen to argue for a probable original date of c.1155–65 for the lost Legendary (1970, 59). Stylistically, the saga-like terseness and detail of the stories contained in this leaf contrast with the accounts in the *Passio Olavi* and the *Old Norwegian Homily Book*, as well as with the second leaf of AM 325, which contains a florid account of the repentance of a sinful young man on seeing a procession of St Óláfr's relics (also found in the *Passio Olavi*, 48/17–50/26 below). The two fragments of AM 325 are in the same hand, but the stylistic difference suggests that they were probably not derived from the same text.

The first twenty-one miracle stories in the Latin *Passio Olavi* (up to and including the healing of a Norwegian king, and including all the miracles in the shorter *Acta Olavi*) appear in a vernacular translation together with a brief Life of St Óláfr in the *Old Norwegian Homily Book* preserved in MS AM 619 4to (ed. Flom 1929, 162–77; *Hom.* 108–29). This manuscript probably dates from c.1200 (Flom 1929, 14; *Hom.* *38–*39). Although a translation, the *Norwegian Homily Book* text is the fullest and best witness to the form the shorter *Acta Olavi* took before it was divided up into lections for liturgical offices, and was accordingly used as a guide by Storm when reconstructing the *Acta Olavi* from breviary texts.

Examination of the relationship between these vernacular texts and the *Acta/Passio Olavi* has established that the shorter Latin text was produced before the longer. The material which *Geisli*, the *Old Norwegian Homily Book* and the *Acta* and *Passio Olavi* have in common suggests that by 1152/3 (the date of *Geisli*) there already existed a text which served as the basis for the first part of the *Homily Book* text and the first part of the *Passio Olavi*; this would have contained the miracle stories which these texts share with *Geisli* (i. e. the first eight or nine, those up to and including the healing of a mutilated English priest, 39/21 below), plus the concluding clause in the Helsinki manuscript discussed by Malin (1920) and now found after miracle XX in the *Old Norwegian Homily Book* (Holtsmark 1956, 20). Ekrem has recently suggested that this earliest collection of miracle stories, which must date from before 1152/3, could originally have appeared at the end of a lost second book of the *Historia Norwegiae*; the high proportion of miracles occurring outside Norway in this section then becomes understandable in the light of Ekrem's suggestion that the *Historia Norwegiae* was written in support of the establishment of a Norwegian archbishopric, since such miracles might carry more weight with the papacy and its advisers (Ekrem 1998a, 83–85).

Holtsmark draws attention to a number of discrepancies between the *vita* section of the *Acta/Passio Olavi* and that of the the *Old Norwegian Homily Book* which suggest that the latter cannot have been a direct translation of the former (1956, 20–22). She concludes that the Norse text must be translated from an earlier version of the *vita* which was also the source for the version which now survives in the *Acta/Passio Olavi* (1956, 22). There are not, however, the same kind of discrepancies between the *miracula* section of the Latin text and the translation of the miracle stories in the *Old Norwegian Homily Book*. Holtsmark's view, then, is as follows: at some date between 1031 (the year of Óláfr's translation) and 1152/3 (the celebrations in Niðaróss marking the establishment of the archiepiscopal see) a **vita* and a **miracula* (containing the miracles up to and including the healing of a mutilated English priest in the present *Passio Olavi*) were written down (1956, 23). Einarr Skúlason appears to draw on this material in *Geisli*; it may have been connected with the **Translatio Olavi* to which Theodoricus is believed to refer. A translation of this **vita* and **miracula* comprises the first part of the *Homily Book* text. The **miracula* section was subsequently expanded to miracle number XX (the healing of a Norwegian king, 52/15–53/5 below), and a translation of these additional miracles is also now found in the *Old Norwegian Homily Book*. The Latin of the *vita* was subsequently revised and the original version lost, so that we now have only the revised Latin text for the *vita* which differs from the vernacular version in the *Old Norwegian Homily Book*.

Some elements of Holtsmark's account are disputed by Erik Gunnes. He agrees (1973, 3) that an initial miracle collection included the first eight miracles (or nine counting the dream at Stiklarstaðir), but argues that this was later extended not to miracle twenty or twenty-one (i.e. the end of the collection in the *Old Norwegian Homily Book,* and in the *Acta Olavi*—so far as we can tell given that the end of this text is lost), but to the end of the twenty-fourth (or twenty-fifth) miracle, the release from an iron band of the two French fratricides and matricides (54/24 below). The sentence at this point beginning 'Preterea, licet tediosa . . .' (Metcalfe 1881, 97) then marks the beginning of a new section:

> Henceforth, although the prolix narrative may seem tedious at times and the unpolished diction may weigh upon the listener, nevertheless, trusting to the devotion of your piety we shall make known to your charity, in a few words, some of those things that we know have been done in recent times (54/27–32 below).

Gunnes also holds that the discrepancies which Holtsmark notes between the *vita* of the *Old Norwegian Homily Book* and that of the *Passio Olavi* are insufficient grounds for positing an earlier, now lost, Latin version of the *vita* by someone other than Eysteinn. He believes that the discrepancies may be explained as adaptations of Eysteinn's Latin by the Norse translator or as the result of later revisions by Eysteinn, rather than by positing a version in which Eysteinn had no involvement (1973, 3–4, 10). He dates Eysteinn's composition of the *vita* to the 1160s and suggests that he revised it in exile when he added the miracles found only in the longer *Passio Olavi.* The revised *vita* then became the basis for all known liturgical offices (1973, 7; cf. 1996, 214; it is not clear why the extra miracles were not widely circulated when the revised *vita* was). Gunnes also argues that there is no reason to believe that Eysteinn was not responsible for the whole text of the *miracula,* including the section translated into the vernacular (1973, 5).

Stylistic studies have helped to determine the extent of Eysteinn's involvement in the extant *Acta Olavi* and *Passio Olavi* (for more information on style than it is appropriate to give here the reader should consult Skard's exhaustive study (1932)). In what follows it will be convenient to refer to the section of the *Passio et miracula Olavi* corresponding to the whole of the *Acta Olavi* (but including the five stories missing in Storm's edition) as A (26/1–53/5 below), the extra miracles up to the 'additional treatise' as B (53/6–61/18), and the additional treatise as C (61/19 to the end). The following table may make matters clearer:

A	Corresponds to contents of *Acta Olavi* and of the *Old Norwegian Homily Book* translation	{	*Vita* 26/1–31/28
			Miracula* 32/1–39/21
			Miracula† 39/22–53/5
B	Further miracles added when the text was revised		*Miracula* 53/6–61/18
C	The 'additional treatise' by Bishop Eysteinn		*Miracula* 61/19–end

* Stories contained in the earliest miracle collection; all but one are also in *Geisli.*
† This section perhaps extends to 54/24 (see Gunnes 1973, 3).

Bang explained the origins of the Latin text(s) by positing a three-stage process of composition based on the collection of stories at Niðaróss and involving three separate authors or redactors producing sections A, B, and C (1912, 59). Malin held that the *Acta Olavi* (corresponding to A) was earlier than the longer *Passio Olavi* (including also B and C) and argued on stylistic grounds that Archbishop Eysteinn was responsible for both the shorter and longer versions (1920, especially 16–27). In a review of Malin's work, Bull (1924) agreed with Malin's views on priority but disagreed with his position on authorship. He held that Eysteinn was certainly responsible for C and could also have written B, adding both to an already existing A. But he, like Bang, believed that it was more natural to attribute A, B and C to three separate authors. The stylistic arguments of Malin and Metcalfe in favour of single authorship for the whole work are, however, corroborated and strengthened by Skard's *Sprache und Stil der Passio Olavi* (1932). Skard agues that the slight differences in style between the earlier and later parts of the work are insufficient to ascribe them to different authors. Important stylistic features found throughout the work include synonymous nouns being used for rhetorical *variatio,* the influence of the Latin Vulgate version of the Bible, and a number of Virgilian echoes (mainly of the *Aeneid* but also of the *Georgics*) which Skard maintains demonstrate first-hand knowledge of the Roman poet's work rather than acquaintance with medieval *florilegia* (1932, 76).[24]

[24] The more significant biblical and Virgilian allusions are referred to in the notes below, but for exhaustive lists the reader should consult Skard 1932, 68–76.

If we accept that Eysteinn was responsible for the whole of the *Passio et miracula beati Olavi*, the tripartite structure of the miracle collection suggests that Eysteinn first produced A, either by collecting together older traditions or by revising an existing text, perhaps adding miracles to a brief collection which had also been used by the poet of *Geisli*. At a later date Eysteinn added additional more recent miracles (B) and then added an original account of further miracles to which he could personally bear witness (C).

Holtsmark argues that Eysteinn may have revised an older Latin text (which she believes had already been translated into Norse) to produce the *Acta Olavi* in the 1060s, shortly after becoming archbishop. Gunnes dates Eysteinn's composition of the *vita* to the same period. Eysteinn's later extensive expansion of the text, adding both B and C, was probably undertaken during his exile in England between 1180 and 1183. On returning to Norway he would have left a text of this expanded *Passio et miracula Olavi* behind in England, where it was copied *c*.1200 into the manuscript belonging now to Corpus Christi College, Oxford.[25] This 'final' version of the *Passio* appears not to have become known outside Britain until it attracted the attention of scholars in the nineteenth century (it is not clear why this fullest surviving version lacks the miracle involving the English knight found in the Helsinki, Douai, Rawlinson and Bordesholm manuscripts). Such a dating of the stages of the genesis of the *Passio Olavi* explains the slight stylistic differences between the earlier and later parts of the work as due to the fact that Eysteinn worked on the first part as a young man, newly made archbishop, but added the later part during his exile some twenty years later.

Although there has been debate and disagreement about the 'prehistory' of the *Passio et miracula beati Olavi,* and about the precise extent of Eysteinn's involvement in the earliest forms of the text, there is a scholarly consensus that the text in Corpus Christi College Oxford MS 209 edited by Metcalfe and translated here is, in this form,

---

[25] The now lost *Vita S. Olaui* referred to in a catalogue of manuscripts at Rievaulx Abbey, now Jesus College, Cambridge MS 34, may have been another copy of Eysteinn's text (cf. Dickins 1937–45, 59).

Eysteinn's work and probably dates from his exile in England, 1180–83. Recent work by Mortensen (2000a) and Ekrem (2000), however, challenges this consensus and questions Skard's arguments in favour of single authorship of the whole text. Mortensen's comparison with the better attested growth of the collections of miracles of Anno of Cologne and Thomas Becket stresses the institutional role in the development of such collections and he even doubts whether Eysteinn was responsible for the whole of the additional treatise (2000a, 101 n. 18). Ekrem argues that the text went through four stages: a short *vita* and the miracles in 32/1–39/21 below, then a revised longer *vita* and the addition of the miracles to 54/24, then the addition of the remainder of B and finally C, with Eysteinn's involvement limited to this final stage (any connection between *Historia Norwegiae* and *Passio Olavi* of the kind Ekrem suggested in her earlier work would then have involved the compiler of the first version of the *Passio Olavi*, and not Eysteinn; cf. Ekrem 2000, 143–54).

At this point, it will perhaps be helpful to discuss briefly the relationship of the texts we have been considering to some important later Norwegian and Icelandic accounts of St Óláfr. Both the 'ecclesiastical' tradition of the *Acta/Passio Olavi* and *Old Norwegian Homily Book* and a more saga-like tradition seem to have fed into the earliest Norse saga of St Óláfr which survives complete, the so-called *Legendary Saga of St Óláfr*. This work is either Norwegian, or Icelandic with Norwegian interpolations: it survives only in a Norwegian manuscript of *c.*1250 (Uppsala Universitetsbibliotek, DG 8; see Jónas Kristjánsson 1976, 281), but originally dates from the early thirteenth century (Jónas Kristjánsson 1976, 293) or *c.*1200 (*Ólhelg(Leg)* 20). Since Louis-Jensen's demonstration that the seventh and eighth fragments printed in Storm's edition of the so-called *Oldest Saga of St Óláfr* do not belong with the remaining six fragments in Oslo, Riksarkivet MS 52 (dated to *c.*1225) it has become clear that the *Oldest Saga* and the *Legendary Saga* are essentially two versions of the same text (Jónas Kristjánsson 1976, 292–93), the latter slightly abbreviating the former while also adding some new material, including a collection of posthumous miracles at the end of the saga which is very similar to the collection translated from Latin in the *Old Norwegian Homily*

Book.[26] In addition to these posthumous miracles the *Legendary Saga* also contains accounts of a number of miracles performed by Óláfr during his life which are not found in the 'ecclesiastical' tradition represented by the *Old Norwegian Homily Book* and *Passio Olavi*. The account of the life of St Óláfr by Snorri Sturluson (1178/9–1241) survives both as a separate saga (*SepÓlhelg*) and as the central third of *Heimskringla*, the great series of Kings' Sagas covering Norwegian history from its mythical past to the reign of Magnús Erlingsson which Snorri probably completed around 1235. The miracle stories which are collected at the end of the *Separate Saga of St Óláfr* appear almost unchanged and in almost the same order in *Heimskringla*, but there they are dispersed throughout the sagas of Óláfr's successors. Snorri's Life of St Óláfr became the basis for later versions in compilations of Kings' Sagas where it was supplemented with material from other sources.

Snorri's sources for Óláfr's miracle stories and his treatment of them are discussed by Whaley (1987, 326–32; cf. also Jørgensen 2000). Snorri seems to have known both a text close to the *Old Norwegian Homily Book* and a text with more concrete detail, perhaps the original version of the text now preserved in fragmentary form in AM 325 IV α 4to. Alternatively, he may have known a now lost text which already combined these two traditions: the lost *Lífssaga Óláfs helga* written by the Icelandic cleric Styrmir Kárason in the 1220s may have done this. It is in any case likely that Snorri made use of Styrmir's work since Styrmir and Snorri were good friends. Since, however, Styrmir's saga no longer survives in its original form it is impossible to be certain.[27]

A number of the early histories of Norway cover Óláfr's reign, but unlike the ecclesiastical texts, the *Legendary Saga* and Snorri's

---

[26] An additional miracle and the fact that some stories are repeated suggest that the *Legendary Saga* depends on more than one source for this collection of posthumous miracles, and that the writer knew an earlier version of the *Legendarium* represented by AM 325 IV α 4to, or a text like it (cf. Whaley 1987, 329).

[27] Nordal attempted a reconstruction of Styrmir's saga (1914, 69–133). Excerpts from Styrmir's original are given in *Flat.* III 237–48; others are incorporated into Snorri's *Separate Saga* in *Flat.* and some other manuscripts (see *SepÓlhelg* 683–95).

work these histories do not include extensive collections of miracle stories. Instead they tend to make a brief and generalised reference to the saint's wonder-working powers and recount only one or two miracles which are of importance in the course of later historical events in Norway. Perhaps because they do not involve the shrine at Niðaróss, these miracles do not appear in the ecclesiastical tradition represented by the *Acta/Passio Olavi* and *Old Norwegian Homily Book* or in the fragments of AM 325 IV α 4to. So, the story of Óláfr's miraculous appearance to his son Magnús before the Battle of Hlýrskógsheiðr (1043) and the subsequent victory over the pagan Wends is recounted in *Ágrip* (ch. 38), Theodoricus (ch. 24), *Fsk* (ch. 50), *Msk* 42–43 (and in *Mgóð(Hkr)* chs 27–28) but not in the *Passio Olavi, Old Norwegian Homily Book* or *Legendary Saga*. Similarly, the miraculous release of Haraldr Sigurðarson from prison in Constantinople appears in *Fagrskinna* (ch. 43), as well as in *Heimskringla (Haralds saga Sigurðarsonar* ch. 14), but not in the 'ecclesiastical' texts.

This contrast with 'historical' works invites consideration of the genre of the *Passio Olavi*. As Metcalfe's title suggests, the *Passio et miracula beati Olavi* combines two hagiographic genres: the *passio* (an account of a martyr's death) and the *miracula* (a collection of miracle stories bearing witness to a saint's sanctity). In attempting to define hagiography Delehaye writes that 'to be strictly hagiographical [a] document must be of a religious character and aim at edification' (1962, 3). Hagiographic literary conventions were the means to specific religious ends: amendment of life, the veneration and imitation of the saint concerned, and through these the worship of God. Such aims are evident in words at the opening of the *miracula* section of the *Passio Olavi*:

> It is fitting to make brief mention of the many miracles that the Lord has deigned to perform in order to make manifest the merits of the glorious martyr Óláfr, so that the souls of those who hear may be moved to praise and venerate the divine mercy, and that it may be revealed to the faithful what great grace and glory the Lord has bestowed upon his saint. (32/2–8 below)

This statement is typical of the prefatory comments which introduce medieval miracle collections (cf. Ward 1982, 29–32). The miracles attributed to a saint were routinely collected at the saint's shrine for at least a brief period after his or her death (Ward 1982, 33–36). Such collections provided the kind of evidence of the saint's sanctity which was required for canonisation, a process which was conducted locally at first (as with Óláfr), but was increasingly reserved to the papacy during the Middle Ages (on the history of the canonisation process see Kemp 1948).

Saints' Lives recount the life of a historical figure, yet Smalley describes the Saint's Life as 'a semi-historical genre' (1974, 49). We might say that whereas history is concerned with the past (even when it is making a point about the present), the subject of hagiography is the eternal as it is manifested in history, the nature of God and of salvation as both are revealed in the life of an historical human being. We may distinguish the different approaches of hagiography and history in terms of the two 'master tropes' of metonymy and metaphor which Roman Jakobson identified as what David Lodge calls 'models for two fundamental ways of organising discourse that can be traced in every kind of cultural production' (1988, 31).[28] Non-hagiographic history is organised metonymically, that is, by contiguity, adjacency or association; its conception of time is successive and linear. Hagiography, on the other hand, is organised metaphorically: it works by analogy or resemblance, stressing the similarities between non-contiguous events and people. The saint is portrayed in terms of an appropriate set or paradigm which connects the saint's life with the lives of other saints and of Christ, and the perceived connections between their lives are reflected in similarities between their written Lives.

The stereotypical characterisation employed in hagiography reflects this 'metaphoric' recognition of similarity in difference. Whereas history's preoccupation is with the particular, hagiography's is with the typical. The hagiographer's overriding interest is in an ideal of human behaviour and in God, rather than in the individual human life. Saints' Lives (and miracle stories) are therefore schematised according to various accepted models which ultimately follow patterns found in Scripture:

> It was the overall intention of any hagiographer to demonstrate that his saintly subject belonged indisputably to the universal community

---

[28] See Jakobson and Halle 1956, 53–82; cf. Lodge 1977.

of saints, and this entailed modelling each *vita* closely on those of earlier authors.[29]

It did not even matter if a miracle story was wrongly ascribed to a particular saint; what mattered was that the story should be edifying. Reginald of Canterbury admits in the Preface to his Life of St Malchus that if he came across a good story anywhere he included it, for all things are common in the communion of saints.[30] Hagiographic conventions may therefore reduce the texts' historical reliability, but they offer an insight into the social and religious attitudes of the period of composition. Saints' Lives can provide valuable evidence for historical *mentalité* even when their value as sources for historical facts is negligible.[31]

St Óláfr is the first and perhaps the most important of a number of canonised Scandinavian rulers. Along with Saints Magnús and Rǫgnvaldr, Earls of Orkney, and Saints Knútr Sveinsson and Knútr lávarðr of Denmark, Óláfr stands in a tradition of royal saints which can be traced back from Scandinavia through Anglo-Saxon England to Merovingian Francia, perhaps even to pre-Christian sacral kingship.[32] Hoffmann lists motifs which the legends of St Óláfr share with Anglo-Saxon royal Saints' Lives and concludes that English models clearly influenced the hagiography of St Óláfr (Hoffmann 1975, 80). This is not surprising, given the English influences on the development of Norwegian Christianity in general and Óláfr's cult in particular. Norway was largely Christianised by English clergy under Óláfr Tryggvason and Óláfr Haraldsson, kings who had both spent time in England. Adam of Bremen records how, soon after Óláfr Haraldsson had become king, he

[29] Lapidge 1991, 254; cf. Boyer 1981.

[30] Cf. Lind 1942, 40–41.

[31] Useful discussions of the historical value of medieval hagiography and the attitudes of historians towards it include Aigrain 1953; Delehaye 1962; Heffernan 1988, especially pp. 38–71; and Fouracre 1990.

[32] On sacral kingship see McTurk 1974–77; 1993; 1994–97; on Merovingian royal saints see Graus 1965; on Anglo-Saxon royal saints see Ridyard 1988; Rollason 1983; 1989; Anglo-Saxon involvement in the conversion of Scandinavia is discussed in Abrams 1995; and for an account of Scandinavian royal saints' cults which stresses their place in this tradition see Hoffmann 1975.

imported English priests and bishops to assist in the conversion of Norway (*Gesta Hamm.* II.lvii (55)). Bishop Grímkell, who initiated Óláfr's cult by building a chapel over his grave, declaring him to be a saint and arranging the translation of his uncorrupted body in the year after his death, was among this group of bishops. It is possible that Grímkell began the collection of miracle stories as evidence of the dead king's sanctity. The earliest surviving Scandinavian sources to refer to Óláfr as a saint are by men who had spent time in England, where they could have encountered the English tradition of royal saints (Þórarinn loftunga, Sigvatr Þórðarson, Archbishop Eysteinn); while Eysteinn was in England he stayed at the abbey of the Anglo-Saxon royal martyr St Edmund.

The cult of St Óláfr influenced the development of later Scandinavian royal cults, including those of St Knútr Sveinsson of Denmark and St Eric of Sweden. There is also evidence of literary connections between Scandinavian royal hagiographic texts. Knud Fabricius notes such connections between the *Passio Olavi* and Ailnoth's Life of the Danish royal protomartyr, St Knútr Sveinsson (1917, 379–80; cf. Hoffmann 1975, 124). Skard maintains that Ailnoth's work influenced the opening of Eysteinn's work (1930–33, 367–68; but cf. Gunnes 1996, 213).

An examination of the kinds of miracles which Óláfr is said to have performed reveals clearly the influence of the typological models of the Saint's Life genre and of the specific hagiographic tradition of royal saints to which Óláfr belongs. Almost all the miracles in the *Passio et miracula beati Olavi* occur after Óláfr's death. The exceptions are his dream before the Battle of Stiklarstaðir (32/9–21) and the story of his hand remaining unharmed when he burned wood-chippings in it which he had made on a Sunday (39/22–40/13). Other texts, for example the *Legendary Saga,* attribute more miracles to Óláfr's lifetime. Robert Folz's comparative study of European royal saints demonstrates that it is not at all unusual for a royal saint to have few miracles attributed to the period during which he was alive on earth (1984, 117–21). Folz also shows that healings always account for the majority of a royal saint's miracles (1984, 128–30), and this is certainly true of the *miracula* of St Óláfr. The influence of hagiographic conventions stemming from the Bible becomes clear when we compare the miracles attributed to Óláfr with the words of Matthew 11: 5:

> Caeci vident; claudi ambulant; leprosi mundantur; surdi audiunt; mortui resurgunt; pauperes evangelizantur.

> The blind see, the lame walk, the lepers are cleansed, the deaf hear, the dead rise again, the poor have the gospel preached to them.[33]

Other types of miracle performed by Óláfr which are commonplace in medieval *miracula* include a number of instances where he protects buildings or people from fire, and two examples of his granting assistance in battle. Often there is some kind of thematic link between miracles in the collection; examples of subject-matter shared by adjacent miracles include the two battles, several miracles involving the healing of people whose tongues had been cut out and miracles associated with liturgical processions. Because the aim of the *miracula* is to encourage devotion to God and his saint rather than to provide historical information for scholars, the miracle stories generally lack specific details such as the names of those involved or the date of the miracle; in some cases these details are provided by other versions of the stories.

The contexts in which the stories of Óláfr's miracles are preserved can be indicative of the functions which they served. The heading over the vernacular Life of Óláfr in the *Old Norwegian Homily Book*, 'In die sancti Olavi regis et martiris' (*Hom.* 108; 'On the Feast Day of St Óláfr, king and martyr'), and its inclusion in a collection of homilies suggest that this version was intended for recitation on Óláfr's feast day, 29 July. The *Acta Olavi* is preserved in breviaries as a series of lessons for offices on 29 July, although Storm (1880, xxxv) pointed out that in some ways the miracle stories might be more appropriate to the feast of Óláfr's Translation, 3 August. Occasional references in the *Passio Olavi* to a listening audience suggest that it too was originally designed for public recitation; two apostrophes to 'brothers' imply a monastic audience (72/18, 73/31).

---

[33] These words which Jesus uses of himself in turn echo Isaiah 35: 5–6.

A HISTORY OF NORWAY

AND

THE PASSION AND MIRACLES OF THE BLESSED ÓLÁFR

A HISTORY OF NORWAY

Here begins the Prologue

. . . tus, treating in his *Philostratus* of the other good things
of life, says in praise of friendship that between true friends 3
hardly any difficulties arise. Not by any means daring to
oppose the well-founded axiom of such a philosopher, knowing
myself incapable of matching in any way such sagacity and 6
my powers too feeble for such an onerous task, yet bound
in duty to respond to the highly honourable urging of the
most excellent of men, lest I show myself ungrateful for the 9
favour of his many generosities, I shall therefore attempt,
willy-nilly, to undertake what is asked of me. For it is a
heavy burden on my ignorant self to describe comprehen- 12
sively the situation of a region so very vast, to disentangle
the genealogy of its rulers, to relate the advent of Christianity side by side with the retreat of paganism and to ex- 15
pound the current state of both religions. You yourself know
best what a labour this will be, full of inordinate toil, a
subject, though hitherto unattempted in Latin discourse, 18
devised by an eminent mind and imposed upon my callow-
ness; and you know best how onerous the task and how
great the risk to be run on account of envious men. I com- 21
ply nevertheless, trusting in the sources we have and dis-
regarding their devouring rancour if it touches us, because
you generations to come will have the fruits of my labour, 24
in which, if the author who obeys has done aught amiss in
untaught presumption, may the patron who ordains par-
don it in forbearing charity. Therefore, Agnellus, whatever 27
other readers may say of these writings of mine, that they
are not smoothed with rhetorical charm but gravelled with
rough barbarisms, do you who are set above me with a 30
teacher's authority receive them with the kindness that befits
a friend. For I am neither eager for praise as a historian

nor fearful of the sting of censure as a liar, since concerning the course of early times I have added nothing new or unknown
3 but in all things followed the assertions of my seniors. On the other hand, if I came upon something noteworthy that occurred in our own day I have included it, for I have ob-
6 served that the illustrious acts of many men, along with the men themselves, daily escape the memory of our contemporaries because there are no writers to record them.

9 *Here begins the first book of the History of Norway*

Norway, then, received its name from a certain king called Nórr. And Norway is a very vast country, though for the
12 most part uninhabitable because of the great number of mountains and forests and frozen tracts. It starts in the east from . . . , a great river, but turns westwards and so
15 by a curving stretch bends its way towards the north. It is a land with many inlets and innumerable promontories and through its length contains three habitable regions. The first
18 and largest is the seaboard region. The second is the interior, also called the mountainous, region. The third is the forest region, lived in by Lapps but not cultivated. Bounded
21 by the stream of ocean to the west and north, it has Denmark and the Baltic Sea to the south, and Sweden, Gautland, Angrmannaland and Jamtaland to the east. Thanks be to
24 God, the populations of these countries are now Christian, but northward and spreading from the east across Norway are many peoples devoted to paganism: Kirjalians,
27 Kvænir, Horn-Lapps and the people of the two Bjarmalands. Of what peoples live beyond these we have no certain knowledge. However, when certain shipmen were trying to re-
30 turn to Norway from Iceland, they were driven by contrary tempests into the wintry region and at last made land between the Greenlanders and the Bjarmians where, so they
33 claimed, they found men of prodigious size and a country

of maidens (these are said to conceive children by a drink of water). Greenland is cut off from these by icy crags. This country, which was discovered, settled and confirmed in the 3 universal faith by Icelanders, is the western boundary of Europe, almost touching the African islands where the waters of ocean flood in. Beyond the Greenlanders some manikins 6 have been found by hunters, who call them Skrælings. Weapon-wounds inflicted on them from which they will survive grow white without bleeding, but if they are mortal the blood 9 hardly ceases flowing. But they lack iron completely: they use whales' teeth for missiles, sharp stones for knives.

Thus far we have made known Norway's situation and 12 surroundings. Now let us also describe its threefold inhabited regions.

The three inhabited parts of Norway   15

The seaboard region can be called Decapolis, for it is famous for ten townships. It comprises four provinces containing twenty-two districts. The first province is called the Vík, 18 beginning at the border of Denmark and extending to the place known as Rýgjarbit; it contains four districts. The second is the Gula province, going as far as the island called 21 Miðja and containing six districts. In the northernmost of these, with the name Mœrr, there is a farm of a marvellous nature, for every felled tree and cut branch turns to 24 stone if they lie one year on the ground there. The third province is called Þrándheimr, a bay with a very narrow entrance, having eight districts in the capacious pouches 27 of its shores and three more outside it, making eleven in all. The fourth is Hálogaland, whose inhabitants often live together with the Lapps and have frequent commerce with 30 them. This province bounds Norway to the north, where the place Vegistafr marks the divide between it and Bjarma-land. The deepest stretch of northern sea is found there, 33

with a Charybdis and Scylla and whirlpools from which
there is no escape; and there are frozen headlands which
3 send headlong into the sea immense icebergs, which are
increased in bulk by the water spewed on them by the flooding
waves and solidified by the frost of winter. Traders making
6 for Greenland often and unwillingly must set their course
among them and so run the risk of shipwreck. There are
also great whales of diverse kind there, shattering the strongest
9 ships and swallowing down the sailors they overwhelm. One-
eyed horse-whales with spreading manes are found there,
most ferocious beasts ploughing the depths of the sea. The
12 *pistrix* is among them and the *hafstrambr*, a monster of
great size but without tail or head, looking like a tree-trunk
as it leaps up and down and portending perils to mariners
15 when it appears. The *hafgufa* and the *hafrkitti* occur there,
the biggest of all sea-monsters, and countless more of this sort.
    Leaving the seaboard, let us move to the mountainous
18 region.

The mountainous parts of Norway

The interior region goes from the border of Gautland and
21 extends to Þrándheimr, comprising four provinces and twelve
districts. The first of these provinces consists of the people
of Raumaríki and Hringaríki in their sequent districts. The
24 second comprises Þelamǫrk and the settlements beyond it.
The third is Heiðmǫrk with the Alv valleys. And the fourth
takes in Guðbrandsdalar with the people of Lóar and other
27 adjacent districts. It ends with the great Dofrafjall. There
are in addition numerous inhabited parts between the seaboard and mountainous regions, Valdres and Haddingjadalr
30 and others, which are subject to the Gulaþing laws. In the
mountainous region there is a river, red with golden sands,
which flows out of the great lake Mjǫrs and reaches the
33 sea in the Vík. Saxons came there once upon a time and

they realised the presence of gold from what they saw on
the hooves of cattle swimming across that river. They secretly
smelted the gold and carried it away in boundless quan-   3
tity. And close to the township of Oslo there is a great wealth
of silver, but floods of water now make it inaccessible to
men and it lies hidden under cliffs of rock.   6
   Now that we have traversed the mountainous region, let
us enter and explore the forests of the Lapps.

The Lapps   9

Bordering the length of Norway is a vast wasteland, separating it from the pagan peoples. This waste is lived in by
Lapps and by the wild animals whose flesh they eat half-   12
raw and whose skins they wear. They are indeed most skilful
hunters, solitary rovers and nomadic. For homes they use
huts of hide which they carry about on their shoulders as 15
they move with their wives and children, travelling faster
than a bird over snow-fields and mountain slopes by means
of smooth wooden slats attached under their feet (a device 18
they call *ondros*) and drawn by reindeer. For where they
lodge is uncertain since at any given time it is the supply of
game which decides their hunting-grounds. There is no limit 21
to the number of wild animals there: bears, wolves, lynxes,
foxes, sables, otters, badgers and beavers. This last beast,
the beaver, is marvellously wary. Since it is very often chased 24
by hunters' hounds, it digs itself three underground dens
by a stream. When the water rises, it keeps to the middle
or top one, but when the water is low and dogs are snap-   27
ping, they leave a slave-beaver in the way of the hounds at
the entrance, and the master-beaver, as if homeward bound,
makes his way with mate and cubs to the lowest den, where 30
he has freer access to the stream, for they put more trust
in travel by water than by land. When winter provisions
are to be gathered in, they work all the harder, using their 33

teeth to cut down huge elms (whose bark is the food they prefer) and load them on their slave, who lies on his back holding a bar of wood in his front paws. They use him as a cart in this way and bring in a great quantity, helping each other to drag the load-bearer by gripping the bar with their teeth. For there is a certain servile class of beaver which fetches a very small price and on account of frequent use for work is not furry but smooth-skinned. Among the Lapps are also a great many squirrels and ermines, and every year the Lapps pay the skins of all these animals as large tribute to the kings of Norway, whose subjects they are.

Their intolerable ungodliness will hardly seem credible nor how much devilish superstition they exercise in the art of magic. For some of them are revered as soothsayers by the foolish multitude because whenever asked they can employ an unclean spirit, which they call a *gandus*, and make many predictions for many people which later come to pass. By marvellous means they can also draw to them- selves objects of desire from distant parts and although far off themselves miraculously bring hidden treasures to light.

Once when some Christians were among the Lapps on a trading trip, they were sitting at table when their hostess suddenly collapsed and died. The Christians were sorely grieved but the Lapps, who were not at all sorrowful, told them that she was not dead but had been snatched away by the *gandi* of rivals and that they themselves would soon retrieve her. Then a wizard spread out a cloth under which he made himself ready for unholy magic incantations and with hands extended lifted up a small vessel like a sieve, which was covered with images of whales and reindeer with harness and little skis, even a little boat with oars. The devilish *gandus* would use these means of transport over heights of snow, across slopes of mountains and through depths of lakes. After dancing there for a very long time

to endow this equipment with magic power, he at last fell
to the ground, as black as an Ethiopian and foaming at the
mouth like a madman, then his belly burst and finally with
a great cry he gave up the ghost. Then they consulted another
man, one highly skilled in the magic art, as to what should
be done about the two of them. He went through the same
motions but with a different outcome, for the hostess rose
up unharmed. And he told them that the dead wizard had
perished in the following way: his *gandus*, in the shape of
a whale, was rushing at speed through a certain lake when
by evil chance it met an enemy *gandus* in the shape of sharp-
ened stakes, and these stakes, hidden in the depths of that
same lake, pierced its belly, as was evident from the dead
wizard in the house.

On another occasion, when Lapps side by side with Christians were trying to hook the squamous flock, the Lapps
had noticed creels almost full of fish in the dwellings of
the Christians, and these they drew from the water's depth
and almost filled their boat with fish.

I have selected these piecemeal from among the innumerable deceptions of the Lapps and offered them as illus-
trations of such a godless group for the benefit of people
who live at a greater distance from them.

Having made the circuit of Norway's regions, let us turn
to the tributary islands. As for the islands which lie off the
coast of Norway itself, they are such a multitude that no
one can count them.

The tributary islands

There are, then, certain islands lying off the coast of the
Gula province which are called the Sólund islands by the
inhabitants, from which the sea between Norway and Scotland is named the Sólund Sea. In this sea are the Orkney
islands, more than thirty in number, deriving their name

from a certain earl named Orkan. These islands have been inhabited by various peoples and are now divided into two realms: the southern isles, enhanced by the rule of petty kings, and the northern isles, graced by the rule of earls. Each of them pays no small tribute to the kings of Norway.

The Orkney islands

These islands were first inhabited by the Picts and the Papar. The Picts, who were only a little bigger than pygmies, worked great marvels in city-building each evening and morning, but at noontide they were utterly bereft of their strength and hid for fear in little subterranean dwellings. At that time moreover the islands were not called the Orkneys but Pictland, and this is why still to this day the sea dividing the islands from Scotland is called the Pictland Firth by the local people. The greatest of all whirlpools is to be found there, which engulfs the strongest ships, sucking them in at ebb tide and spewing out their fragments with a belch at flood tide. We do not know at all where these people came from. On the other hand, the Papar got their name from the albs they wore, like clerics, for all clergy are called *papæ* in the German tongue. There is moreover an island still today called Papey after them. It is seen, however, from the character and script of the books they left behind them that they were Africans who practised Judaism. When Haraldr hárfagri ruled in Norway some vikings of the kin of a very mighty prince, Rǫgnvaldr, crossed the Sólund Sea with a large fleet, drove the Papar from their long-established homes, destroyed them utterly and subdued the islands under their own rule. With winter bases thus provided, they sallied forth all the more securely in summer and imposed their harsh sway now on the English, now on the Scots, and sometimes on the Irish, so that Northumbria in England, Caithness in Scotland, Dublin and other coastal towns in Ireland were brought under their rule. In this company was a certain Hrólfr, called Gǫngu-Hrólfr by his comrades because he always travelled on foot, his immense size making it impossible for him to ride. With a few men and by means of a marvellous stratagem he took Rouen, a city in Normandy. He came into a river with fifteen ships, where each crew member dug his part of a trench which was then covered by thin turves, simulating the appearance of firm ground. They then arrayed themselves on the landward side of the trenched ground and advanced prepared for battle. When the townsmen saw this, they met the enemy in head-on attack, but these feigned flight as if racing back to their ships. The mounted men, pursuing them faster than the rest, all fell in heaps into the hidden trenches, their armoured horses with them, where the Norwegians slaughtered them with deadly hand. So, with the flight of the townsmen, they freely entered the city and along with it gained the whole region, which has taken its name of Normandy from them.

Having obtained rule over the realm, this same Hrólfr married the widow of the dead count, by whom he had William, called Longspear, the father of Richard, who also had a son with the same name as himself. The younger Richard was the father of William the Bastard, who conquered the English. He was the father of William Rufus and his brother Henry, who in the prophecies of Merlin is styled the Lion of Justice. When established as count of Normandy Hrólfr invaded the Frisians with a hostile force and won the victory, but soon afterwards he was treacherously killed in Holland by his stepson.

Meanwhile his comrades confirmed their dominion in the Orkney islands, which are indeed to this day still under the rule of their descendants, though subject to the kings of Norway by due payment of tribute.

The Faroe islands

In the streams of ocean there are also 'islands of sheep',
3 eighteen in number, which the inhabitants call Færeyjar in
their native tongue, for fat flocks abound in the ownership
of the farmers there, some having sheep by the thousand.
6 These islanders also pay tribute to our kings at fixed times.

Iceland

Westwards from there is the big island which the Italians
9 called Ultima Thule. It is now inhabited by a multitude of
colonists but it was once a vast empty land and unknown
to men until the time of Haraldr hárfagri. Then Ingólfr and
12 Hjǫrleifr, Norwegians who were fleeing their homeland on
account of killings, took ship with their wives and children
and, seeking their way through the combing waves, finally
15 found the island which had first been discovered by Garðarr
and subsequently by Anbi. In about fifty years it was inhabited all over in the same way as it is today. The Norwe-
18 gians call this island Iceland, 'the land of ice', for the island
contains countless mountains covered with uninterrupted
sheets of ice and by their sheen mariners at sea and far
21 from land customarily set their course for the haven best
suited to them. Among them is Mount Hekla which, quaking all over like Mount Etna, is shaken by a terrible distur-
24 bance of the ground and sends out bursts of sulphurous
flames. Small hot springs similarly boil up at various sites
which, roofed over and tempered by the introduction of cold
27 water, provide the local people with bath-like washing places.
There are some other wells on the island in which wool or
cloth steeped overnight turns to stone. Another spring there,
30 gushing in the sandy coils of a river, has the taste and colour
of beer; a mere mouthful is said to restore health.

Nor do I think it proper to pass over what is reported to
33 have occurred in our own time: for over a stretch of three

miles the whole ocean began to surge like narrow waters
and boil like a cauldron, while out of the deep the gaping
earth sent forth fire-spewing vapours and a great moun-   3
tain emerging from the waves. This will be thought an evil
omen by many people, auguring that when the elements
spontaneously disturb the regular tides and movements of   6
nature it either portends marvels on earth or prefigures the
end of the world. For in the book Solinus wrote on the wonders
of the world, he said that there is a very deep abyss in the   9
earth itself (which is why it is written, 'the fountains of the
great deep were broken up') and alongside it are open-mouthed
caverns containing winds which are said to be brought forth   12
by the breathing of the water, and these are the breath of
gales. Indeed, by their breathing these winds draw to them
the waters of the sea through hidden passages in the earth;   15
they shut them up in the vaults of the abyss, and then by
the same force drive them out again, causing sea-surges,
spates and the whirling of waterspouts. Earthquakes also   18
occur and various discharges of vapour and conflagration,
for when the winds' breath, held in the cheeks of earth, presses
to burst out, it shakes the foundation of the world with a   21
dreadful roaring and forces it to tremble. So when the winds'
breath contends with fire in the earth's interior, then even
in mid-ocean the depths are fissured and smoky exhalations   24
and sulphurous flames are seen to emerge. Similarly, what
is a tremor in the ground is believed to correspond to thunder
in the clouds, a rift here to lightning there. Although we do 27
not clearly understand these marvels in the world, or others greater still, they are not therefore to be taken as omens
or reckoned portents foreboding the deluge. On the con-   30
trary, since in some mysterious manner they gloriously serve
him who knows all things unknown, the immutable Creator of mutable things, they comply with nature in every way. 33
Since, truly, the spark of our feeble intellect, surrounded

by the obscurity of corporeal darkness, is found quite incapable of investigating the deepest causes, let us call for
3 enlightenment on him who with the spirit of understanding brings to light the things hidden in darkness.
So far we have described the tributary islands one by
6 one. Let us now, however, turn our pen to an account of the kings who have ruled Norway and from whom they descend.

The origin of the kings

9 The ancient line of the kings of Norway had its beginning in Sweden, from where Þrándheimr, the principal region of Norway, was also settled. So King Ingvi, whom many
12 assert to have been the first to rule the kingdom of Sweden, fathered Njǫrðr, who fathered Freyr—both these were worshipped as gods by their posterity through many cen-
15 turies. Freyr fathered Fjǫlnir, who was drowned in a vat of mead and whose son, Svegðir, chased a dwarf into a rock and is said never to have returned, which can cer-
18 tainly be counted a fable. He fathered Vanlandi, who was smothered by a demon in his sleep and died. This sort of demon is called *mara* in Norwegian. Vanlandi fathered
21 Vísburr, who with all his retinue was burned alive by his sons so that they might all the sooner inherit the kingdom. His son, Dómaldi, was hanged by the Swedes as a sacri-
24 fice to the goddess Ceres to ensure the fertility of the crops. He fathered Dómarr who died of sickness in Sweden and whose son, Dyggvi, also ended his life in that country. His
27 son Dagr succeeded him in the reign; Danes killed him in a general battle at a ford called Skjótansvað or Vápnavað when he was seeking to avenge a sparrow's wrongs. He
30 fathered Alrekr who was beaten to death with a bridle by his brother, Eiríkr. Alrekr was the father of Hǫgni, whose wife killed him with her own hands, hanging him from a
33 tree by a golden chain at the place Agnafit, which is now

called Stockholm. His son, Ingjaldr, was killed in Sweden by his own brother because of the taunting of the latter's wife; her name was Bera (which is *ursa* in Latin). After him came his son, Jǫrundr, who met a miserable end when he fought against the Danes and was hanged by them on the sea-inlet in Denmark which the natives call Limafjǫrðr. He was the father of Aun who, it is told, in the drawn-out infirmity of old age took no solid food for nine years before his death but only sucked milk from a horn like an infant. Aun fathered Egill, nicknamed Vendilkráki, who was deprived of his kingdom by his own slave, named Tunni. The slave raised civil strife against his master in eight battles and won the victory in all of them; he fell in the ninth, vanquished at last, but the king himself was soon afterwards gored to death by a ferocious bull. He was succeeded in the realm by his son Óttarr who was killed by a namesake, Óttarr, earl of the Danes, and Fasti, his brother, in Vendill, one of the provinces of Denmark. His son Aðils, or Aðísl, fleeing from idolatrous sacrifice, fell from his horse in front of the temple of Diana and died. He was father of Eysteinn, whom the Gautar forced into a house and burnt alive with his men. His son Yngvarr, nicknamed 'the White', was killed in a campaign on an island in the Baltic Sea which is called Eysýsla by the natives. This Yngvarr fathered Braut-Qnundr who was killed by his brother, Sigvarðr, at Himinheiðr, whose name means 'field of heaven'. In succession to him his son Ingjaldr was elevated to the kingship. He had immoderate fear of a King Ívarr, called *víðfaðmi*, who terrified many people at the time, so with all his retinue he shut himself up in his feasting-hall and set it on fire. His son Óláfr, with the nickname 'Tree-feller', ruled the kingdom long and peacefully and died full of days in Sweden.

Óláfr was the father of Hálfdan, with the nickname 'White-leg', whom the Norwegians of the mountainous region

accepted as king when he came from Sweden. He gave up
the ghost at an advanced age in the district of Þótn.
When his son Eysteinn, nicknamed 'Fart', was sailing in narrow
waters between two islands with many ships in company,
he was knocked off the stern-deck by a spar from another
vessel and disappeared, sunk beneath the waves. He was
succeeded by his son Hálfdan who was lavish of gold and
most tenaciously sparing of food, for he presented his retainers with gold and tortured them with hunger. He was
the father of Guðrøðr the Hunter-king who was betrayed
by his own wife, for a young man whom she bribed pierced his
side with a spear. His son Hálfdan, nicknamed 'the Black',
likewise held the kingdom in the mountainous region after
his father. On his way from a feast, when he was travelling with wagons and many mounted men across the ice
of a lake called Rǫnd, he was carelessly driven into a break
in the frozen surface, where herdsmen customarily watered
their beasts, and perished under the ice.

His son who succeeded him, Haraldr hárfagri, so called
because of his comely head of hair, was the first to hold
sway over the whole seaboard region; indeed, the interior
region, hitherto ruled by petty kings, was likewise as good
as under his rule. Many and marvellous are the things told
of him, which it would take too long to rehearse in sequence
at this point. He ruled for seventy-three years and had sixteen sons. The first-born was Eiríkr, nicknamed *blóðøx*,
that is 'bloody axe'. The second was Hákon, whom Æthelstan,
king of the English, adopted as a son. The third Óláfr. The
fourth Bjǫrn, which means 'bear'. The fifth Sigvarðr, nicknamed 'the Giant'. The sixth Gunnrøðr. The seventh Guðrøðr.
The eighth Hálfdan High-leg. The ninth Rǫgnvaldr réttilbeini, who was fostered by a sorceress in the district of
Haðaland and was active in the same magic art as his
foster-mother. The tenth was Eysteinn. The eleventh Jǫrundr.

The twelfth Sigtryggr. The thirteenth Yngvarr. The four-
teenth Tryggvi. The fifteenth Hringr. The sixteenth Hrólfr.
The oldest of these, Eiríkr Bloodaxe, acquired the king-   3
dom after his father and took to wife a vicious and most
iniquitous woman from Denmark named Gunnhildr, the
daughter of the notably foolish Gormr, king of the Danes, and   6
of the notably sagacious woman, Þyri. With Gunnhildr he
had six sons, namely Haraldr, with the nickname 'Greypelt',
second Gamli, third Sigvarðr Gleam, fourth Gunnrøðr, fifth   9
Erlingr, sixth Gormr. After ruling for a year, and pleasing
no one on account of the excessive arrogance of his wife,
Eiríkr was deprived of the kingdom by his brother Hákon,   12
foster-son of Æthelstan, king of England, with the agreement of the chief men of Norway, and Eiríkr withdrew as
a fugitive to England. There he was well received by his   15
brother's foster-father and laved in the fount of baptism;
he was made earl over all Northumbria and proved most
acceptable to all until his outrageous wife, Gunnhildr,   18
arrived. The Northumbrians would not suffer her pestilential
fury and forthwith threw off their intolerable yoke. Eiríkr,
however, died when he was attacked while on a foray in   21
Spain, and Gunnhildr returned with her sons to her brother
Haraldr, king of the Danes.

Hákon was accepted as king by the seaboard peoples of   24
Norway. This man, most dutifully reared by a most Christian king in England, nevertheless went so far astray that
by a most wretched exchange he preferred an ephemeral   27
realm to the eternal kingdom. In his anxiety to retain his
sovereign rank he became, alas, an apostate, subject in servi-
tude to idols, serving gods, not God. But although eternally   30
deprived of perdurable greatness because of blind ambi-
tion for fleeting majesty, he nevertheless observed his nation's
laws and the decisions of the people more faithfully than   33
all the kings who lived in the heathen age. Because of this

he was indeed dear to the nobility and an object of devotion to the commoners. He defended his homeland with
3 the utmost vigour for twenty-seven years. In the last years of his life he was engaged in almost constant warfare against his nephews, the sons of his brother and Gunnhildr, their
6 mother. Two of their battles were especially renowned. One was at the place called Rastarkálfr on the island of Frædi in the district of Norð-Mœrr, where Gamli, son of Gunnhildr,
9 and a great number of their host were forced off a promontory into the sea. The other great battle they fought was in the Gula province at the settlement called Fitjar, an
12 encounter in which many fell on both sides. Two sons of Gunnhildr, Gormr and Erlingr, fell there, while their other brothers fled. But in their retreat a lad in their company
15 threw a spear aimed at the battle-line of the enemy which gave King Hákon himself a lethal wound in his upper arm on the right side. It will be clearly apparent to all and sun-
18 dry that it was divine vengeance that brought about this event in such a way: having dared to deny the Christ Child, he was now overcome by a mere boy after his enemies were
21 defeated. He decided to return to his estate of Alreksstaðir but he died on the way in the very haven where he had been born, and as a result this place has ever since been
24 called Hákonarhella, that is 'Hákon's stone'.

After these events the whole seaboard region was held for fourteen years by Gunnhildr and her sons, Haraldr,
27 Sigvarðr and Gunnrøðr. Under their rule Norway was most heavily oppressed by famine and all sorts of evils through the exceptional wickedness of its rulers. But Sigvarðr and
30 many other men were killed at an assembly by the people of Vǫrs, led by Vémundr vǫlubrjótr. Gunnrøðr, however, was killed on the Alreksstaðir estate (the famous town of
33 Bergen is now situated nearby) by a certain Þorkell, nicknamed *klyppr*, whose wife he had ravished against her will.

He thrust him through with a sword, and one of his retainers, Erlingr the Old by name, manfully avenged him. But . . . Of the great number of Haraldr hárfagri's sons two, that 3 is Eiríkr and Hákon, are said to have ruled the seaboard peoples in succession to their father; the others had rule in the mountainous region. Some indeed ended their lives 6 before their time to rule arrived, for Hálfdan High-leg was killed by the Orkney islanders, while Rǫgnvaldr réttilbeini, infamous for the disgrace customarily attached to degrad- 9 ing practices, is said to have been thrown into a whirlpool in Haðaland on his father's orders. But their brothers left to pos- terity an altogether worthy lineage, for from their line sprang 12 those two health-bringing namesakes, Óláfr and Óláfr, who, like bright lights of heaven, illumined their homeland with the radiance of holy faith. Bjǫrn, son of Haraldr hárfagri, 15 was nurtured in Grenland, where he is also said to have ruled. He fathered Guðrøðr who was the father of Haraldr the Grenlander, who was brought up and had rule in Grenland. 18 He made a very choice match with Ásta, daughter of Guðbrandr kúla, and she bore him Óláfr, perpetual king of Norway. Sigvarðr Sow, king in the mountainous region, 21 took Ásta in marriage after the death of her husband. Sigvarðr risi (that is, 'the Giant'), son of Haraldr hárfagri, was the father of Hálfdan who was the father of Sigvarðr Sow. By 24 Ásta he had Haraldr, a man of great sagacity and deep experience in the art of war. The fabric of the genealogy of the kings of Norway, stretching down to this day, de- 27 scends from him, as it were by a thread. Óláfr, son of Haraldr hárfagri, was the father of Tryggvi. Tryggvi, nurtured in Raumaríki, where he is said to have first had rule, married 30 Ástríðr, a lovely maiden from the mountainous region. Later, when he had subjugated the Vík, he was cunningly led astray and treacherously killed by his cousins, namely the 33 sons of Eiríkr, in a small island in Ranríki on an occasion

when they were supposed to confirm a pact of peace betwen
them. That place is still called Tryggvareyrr, that is 'Tryggvi's
3 cairn'. Many people maintain that Tryggvi's death came
about in this different way: when the local people, that is
the men of Ranríki, had no stomach to tolerate the harsh-
6 ness of his rule, an assembly was summoned, as if for the
public weal, at which they had the king deceitfully killed
by Saxi, Skorri and Skreyja, youths bribed with money for
9 the purpose. But whether it was done by the first lot or the
second, the name of the site on that island demonstrates
that he was done to death there. Meanwhile Ástríðr her-
12 self, now pregnant, went with three ships and fitting company to the Orkney islands; there she was most loyally given
refuge and there the happy mother-to-be gave birth to the
15 future king, whom she named Óláfr, through whom Norway finally received the most salutary admonitions of Christ.

On the death of the sons of Gunnhildr, a certain Hákon
18 (nicknamed 'the Bad' on account of the unrestrained cruelty
of his nature), who had the title of earl, usurped sovereignty over all Norway after having expelled all the petty
21 kings and done away with those who were tributary to the
Swedes. And he preferred to be called 'earl' like his forebears rather than 'king', for through his father Sigvarðr
24 and his mother Bergljót, daughter of Þórir the Silent, he was
descended from the line of the earls of Mœrr and Hálogaland. Mighty in war but stubbornly devoted to idolatry, he
27 increased his dominion far and wide, subduing numerous
neighbouring regions. But when he learnt of the fatherless boy born in Orkney, he straightway laid crafty plans
30 against the lad who would, he suspected, deprive him of
the kingdom. When his mother learnt of the earl's malevo-
lent plots, then in order to remove the boy from her to safety
33 she gave him, by God's provident mercy (so I believe), although she loved him dearly as her only son, to a certain

Þórólfr Louse-beard to foster and carry to Sweden. Þórólfr took the child as his to foster with every care and carrying him in his bosom passed through Þrándheimr in the greatest peril. After that he got to Sweden, where he paused for a time, then made for Russia but landed in Estonia. In the end while sailing off Eysýsla they were intercepted by pirates and some of them taken prisoner, some killed. Among them the boy's foster-father was also executed, while the boy Óláfr himself was sold as a slave to Estonians. Óláfr was redeemed from there by a kinsman of his who by chance was sent there at that time by the king of Russia with the task of collecting taxes. For some years Óláfr lived privately with him in Russia. When he was about twelve years old he manfully avenged his foster-father in the middle of the market-place of Hólmgarðr, and word of this unheard-of act of vengeance by a lad barely twelve years of age soon reached the king. Because of it he was presented to the king, by whom he was finally adopted as a son. Practising piracy as a youth, traversing the Baltic shores and striking terror into all the peoples of those parts, this glorious bandit was in his ignorance steered away from God. His fleet was swelled by Norwegians and Danes, Gautar and Slavs, who joined him in making their winter quarters in Jómsborg, the strongest of the Slav townships. From here he made for Frisia, after that entered Flanders, and from there went to England, and after ravaging these lands he worked wonders in Scotland and spared no one in Ireland. But indeed the Creator, taking care of his created, in the bowels of his mercy miraculously visited this tyrant so free and fierce, and by his visitation illumined him, so that those whom he had hitherto cloaked in the shadow of death, He might now clothe in the robe of eternal radiance. For when this Óláfr had inflicted his insensate rage on the peoples named he came upon a hermit serving God on a small island off

Britain. Óláfr put him to the test by changing clothes with
his shield-bearer, but he at once recognised this servant
3 of the king and admonished him to serve his lord faithfully. At that the princely leader of pirates made haste to
visit the hermit, who he now had no doubt was a prophet
6 of God, and he heard from him many predictions which
he soon found by experience to be true.

'You will be,' he said, 'an illustrious king, most devout
9 in the Christian faith and most beneficial to your people,
for through you innumerable people will become truly
Christian. And if the things I foretell are true, take this as
12 a sign: the day after tomorrow, when you leave your ships,
you will see cattle on the shore and you will realise that there
is deceit behind it, for you will be ambushed by enemies.
15 But while you are suffering losses among your men, you
yourself will be wounded almost to death and you will be
carried barely alive on a shield to your ships. After a week
18 you will be healed with heaven's help and on your return
you will be laved in the fount of life.'

The outcome verified all these things, just as he fore-
21 told them.

When the blessed Óláfr, through the health-giving change
effected by the right hand of the Most High, had received
24 the grace of baptism, and the greater part of his host with
him, he crossed the sea to Norway, having with him Bishop
Johannes and the priest Þangbrandr whom he sent to preach
27 to the Icelanders. He also had with him many other ministers
of God, all of whom began to preach Christ with one mind
and one mouth to the heathens. The Norwegians, converted
30 to the faith by the measureless mercy of the great God, made
Óláfr their king and expelled Earl Hákon from the realm after
he had been ruling for thirty-three years. A slave of his by
33 the name of Karkr killed him despicably by night in Gaular-
dalr, one of the districts of Þrándheimr, and even brought

his severed head to the king, hoping to win great rewards. But what befell him was just the reverse of that, for he was publicly condemned as a most villainous murderer and hanged as a criminal. But the sons of Earl Hákon, Sveinn and Eiríkr, fled to Denmark and were peacefully received by King Sveinn.

Meanwhile Óláfr reconciled all his countrymen in the seaboard region to the King of Kings, and if there were those whom the bishop could not subdue to the reign of Christ by the sword of the spirit, the king used material means on noble and commoner, suckling child with the man in years. Thus it came about that within five years he rendered to Christ all the peoples of the tributary islands, the Shetlanders, the Orcadians, the Faroese and the Icelanders, shining in faith, rejoicing in hope, ardent in charity. As a result, the chariot of God, multiplied by ten thousand, and the waggon of Christ, filled full of his salvation freely offered, were drawn by this wonder-working king, as if by the strongest horse, to the farthest bounds of the world and set on course to return to the homeland of Paradise.

Óláfr married a lady from Denmark, sister of King Sveinn, Þyri by name, who had in fact been previously betrothed against her will to the duke of Slavland. But because King Sveinn determined to keep fast hold on Sjáland, which he had given in dowry to his sister, King Óláfr went to war against the Danes, and he ordered that a great fleet from Þrándheimr and Gulaþing should be gathered by the leading men; and he himself summoned the host of the eastern region and waited for the others on the border between Denmark and Norway. So, when some of the Gulaþing men arrived, the king set off with no great numbers on the planned expedition, hoping that the rest of the force would follow him. But they were unwilling to cross their country's frontier, especially when their leader had departed, and they went back to their homes. When the king realised that they had cheated him, he decided to go to the Slavs and seek reinforcements from the men who had been his most loyal comrades in piracy. But while sailing past Sjáland, he was cut off by enemies in ambush like a sheep by wolves. The fact was that, when King Sveinn heard that Óláfr would be coming with an armed force, he summoned his stepson, Óláfr king of the Swedes, and Eiríkr, the son of Earl Hákon, and these three against one then fought their sea-battle in this way. First Sveinn attacked Óláfr with thirty ships while he fought back with only eleven, but the royal ship was furnished with eighty bench-divisions. This vessel, which had the image of a serpent's head on prow and stern, was called the Long Serpent. It had room for one hundred and sixty oarsmen if all the half-bench spaces together were occupied for rowing, and in the battle now spoken of all of them are said to have been in coats of mail. There were also forty clerics in the thirty half-bench spaces nearest the stern; not brought up to war, they worked harder at praying than fighting. After a long struggle each one of Sveinn's ships had been cleared of men and he returned with great disgrace to his allies. Then his stepson Óláfr, with the same number of ships, attacked his namesake and suffered worse loss than Sveinn, his predecessor, and retired with great dishonour. Eiríkr, last in sequence but first in victory, made a most fierce attack on the enemy; not unmindful of the death of his father and his own flight, he dealt injuries to pay for those injuries. But Óláfr, as if starting all over again in resisting with all his might the strong onslaught of those bold rebels, strove to hurl stones, spears and other missiles at their adversaries. Finally, with no strength left and their ships boarded by their enemies with no one to lift a hand against them, all those still quickened by the warmth of life were devoured by the sword's mouth, except the king himself who was last seen by them standing on the lofty stern-deck.

But when the battle was over they found him neither alive nor dead, and because of this some say that, being in armour, he sank under the waves. There are others who claim to have seen him long afterwards in a certain monastery. But how he may have been brought through the perils of the sea to the firm ground of the shore—by his own swimming or by a skiff's conveyance or by spirits angelic and attendant—or whether he drowned there is, I believe, unknown to all our contemporaries. Therefore let us more honestly leave the subject by omitting what is indefinite rather than offering false opinion on an uncertain fact. But certainly Óláfr's wife bore the death of her husband with excessive tribulation and died of grief.

After these events rule over all Norway was conceded by Sveinn Forkbeard to the sons of Earl Hákon. They presided over the realm as earls for fourteen years and almost uprooted God's holy church which the blessed Óláfr had planted and Johannes watered.

Óláfr Haraldsson

In those times Óláfr, son of Haraldr the Grenlander, was held in high esteem in Russia. Because he was dispossessed of his native land, he had to turn to piracy. He usually wintered in Eapolis, which we call Hólmgarðr, attended by no small fleet. In summer he constantly harassed all the peoples round the Baltic Sea with raiding and ravaging. He utterly laid waste the large and populous island of Eysýsla, and so harried two others equal to it in size and population, namely Gotland and Eyland, that their inhabitants paid enormous sums in tribute throughout the time he stayed in Russia. In the country of the Kurlanders he inflicted no small slaughter on them, crowned with most glorious success. After long displaying the fierceness of a tyrant, this splendid leader made ready to return to his homeland, but when he arrived in Denmark,

he was invited by Sveinn, king of the Danes, to cross the sea with him to England; Knútr accompanied his father Sveinn.
3 They won the victory in every battle through the military shrewdness of that most blessed tyrant, Óláfr. At last Æthelred was driven out and Sveinn held the whole island but only
6 briefly, for three months later he was removed from the light of this world. When Knútr returned to his homeland, he was made king by the Danes in place of his father. Óláfr
9 meanwhile waged war against the Britons and reached even regions of Spain; leaving there the clearest tokens of his triumph, he returned to Denmark and was received with high
12 honour by his comrade, now king of the Danes. They made a pact of brotherhood by adoption. But because Knútr had fled ingloriously from England on the death of his father, he
15 now intended to return with an enormous army. He strongly urged his comrade Óláfr and his step-brother of the same name to go with him, promising them half if it proved possible
18 for him to win the whole island with their support. Consequently they eagerly started off together and with billowing sails and fair winds in three days reached the port
21 of Yarmouth. From there they moved on to attack London, where by chance King Edmund was staying at the time, now deprived of his father Æthelred. When the king learnt
24 of the arrival of the enemy, he summoned the townsmen and ordered them to fortify the bridge over the River Thames so that his foe should not have free entry. They took ac-
27 tion without delay to fulfil his command, and he gathered a host from the neighbouring districts. Meanwhile the Danes, approaching the bridge with huge clamour, began all with
30 one intent to assault their fortifications, while those on the other side strove with all their might to defend themselves and their property. When Knútr had thus contended all day
33 in fruitless effort and suffered the sore loss of many of his men, our Óláfr put himself and his men into great danger

for the sake of victory. With eleven ships he rowed hard against the bridge defences, his troops covered by protective shields, and risking their lives to make mock of the contrivan-   3
ces of the defenders, they most audaciously penetrated them. When the supremely victorious Óláfr had made his entry into the city, he was accorded splendid acclamations of praise   6
by the whole host, and the renown of the triumph won was attributed all to him. After London was taken they fought hard against King Edmund five times in nine months. At last when   9
both sides were exhausted, the kings, Edmund and Knútr, made a pact by which as long as both lived they should rule the island on equal terms, but the one who outlived the other   12
should have it all. Then when Edmund had reigned for a single month he was deprived of the light of this world and Knútr took possession of the whole kingdom. He married the mother   15
of his late co-regent, named Ælfgifu, who as . . . Sveinn and Knútr, nicknamed 'the Hard', his two sons. The agreement he had most firmly made with his supporters he set entirely   18
at nought, allowing both his brother and his comrade to depart disappointed of all reward for their labours. Before leaving, Óláfr of Norway was then betrothed to the sister of Óláfr   21
of Sweden, Margaret by name, whom he had long esteemed highly with the favour of deep affection becomingly recip-
rocated. But this came to nothing, for she was forced by her   24
brother to marry King Jaroslav of Russia against her will. This act would have fomented very great hatred and discord among those three illustrious princes had not Margaret's   27
exceedingly wise sister, following the counsel of her foster-
father, most fittingly re-knit the severed ties of the previous betrothal: for Óláfr made her his wife and by her had . . .   30
    Óláfr, returning from England with two big ships of burden, crossed the sea to his native Norway. Four bishops were with him, namely Grímkell, Bernard, Ruðólfr and Sigfrid.   33

The end

THE PASSION AND MIRACLES OF THE
BLESSED ÓLÁFR

*Here begins the Passion of the blessed Óláfr, king and
martyr*

3 When the illustrious King Óláfr ruled in Norway, a vast
country located towards the north and having Denmark to
the south, there entered into that land the feet of them that
6 preach the gospel of peace and bring glad tidings of good
things. The peoples of that country, previously subject to
the ungodly rites of idolatry and deluded by superstitious
9 error, now heard of the worship and faith of the true God—
heard indeed, but many scorned to accept. Living in a region close to the north, it was that same north, from which
12 comes every evil over the whole face of earth, that had
possessed them all the more inwardly and gripped them all
the more firmly in the ice of unbelief. From its face Jeremiah
15 saw a seething pot; and in Isaiah there is the boaster who
says, 'I will exalt my throne above the stars of God: I will
sit also upon the mount of the congregation, in the sides
18 of the north.' But the great and praiseworthy Lord, who
builds his city on the sides of the north, scattered the rigour of the north with the mild wind of the south and at last
21 softened the stubborn and fierce hearts of savage peoples
with the warmth of faith. They heard of the teaching of the
Lord, and he sent messengers to them as heralds of his
24 word. They should preach in those parts the truth which is
in Christ Jesus, overthrow the cult of idols, promise un-
failing life and eternal joys to those who believed, and deter
27 the unbelieving and contumacious with the fear of judgement to come and everlasting torment.

Now this kingdom, as we have said, was ruled by King
30 Óláfr. Although a pagan, he was nevertheless benevolent
by nature and from a certain nobility of mind very eager to

follow the ways of righteousness. Having learnt the purity
of Gospel truth in England, he took the faith wholly to
heart and with devout zeal hastened to receive baptismal   3
grace in the city of Rouen. Purified thus at the health-
giving font, he at once became a different man and, as the
apostle said, was buried with Christ by baptism into death.   6
Forgetting what had gone before, passing on to things to
come, this most perfect observant of the faith he had adopted
walked in newness of life. All vain pleasure seemed pal-   9
try to him, and the glory of earthly kingship grew vile in
comparison with heavenly bliss. Although of royal rank,
he was poor in spirit, and though involved in worldly af-   12
fairs, he yet gave his mind to heavenly matters. Whatever
divine law forbids he vehemently rejected; whatever that
law commands he embraced with the most ardent love.   15

Not content with his own salvation, he strove with unflagging urgency to convert the people he was appointed
by divine providence to govern. And by a new order of   18
things, the king played an apostle's part and he, the ruler,
himself preached the grace of the word of Christ to all people
far and wide. Moreover, by the grace poured into his lips, he   21
led not a few away from the abominable worship of demons
to knowledge and veneration of their Creator. His wonderful
devotion and most abstemious life kindled in the hearts of   24
many contempt of this world and love of the heavenly homeland. Whose stubbornness, whose hardness of heart, was
not subdued by the sweet words, full of spiritual wisdom,   27
of the illustrious Óláfr? Whose torpor and sloth were not
roused by his peerless conduct?

Even in the midst of a vicious and perverse nation he   30
made many converts. Yet he also had very many strong and
mighty enemies, who were moved more by wilfulness than
piety, more by custom than reason, more by rash fury of   33
spirit than love of truth. They fought with all their might

against the message and holy works of this most noble martyr of Christ and sought to overthrow the just ways of the Lord.
3 But the righteous man, bold as a lion, was without dread and, following the example of the blessed Job, he did not fear a great multitude nor did the contempt of families ter-
6 rify him. Nor could he be turned from his steadfast preaching by the threats and plots of enemies.

Gracious Jesus, what labours, what persecutions he en-
9 dured before he was able to turn that unbelieving and hostile nation from its perversity! Without doubt, it was given to him not only to believe in Christ but also to suffer for his
12 sake. Not only was he ready to suffer, not only ready to yield up the crown of temporal kingship for Christ's sake, but he also desired to win the glory of everlasting felicity
15 through the crown of martyrdom. Oh, what ardour of devoted love, what fervour of faith, inflamed the breast of this most excellent martyr of Christ, in the midst of savage
18 people who, trusting in their own folly, were in Solomon's words less safe to encounter than a bear robbed of her whelps. Yet whenever he could, in public and in private, he never
21 ceased to pour forth before them the message of faith and salvation which they detested. He accomplished much in a short time and won a countless multitude for the Lord. Peo-
24 ple flocked eagerly to baptism and the number of believers grew day by day. Idols were smashed, sacred groves felled, temples overthrown. Priests were ordained and churches
27 built. The people made offerings with devotion and zeal. The worshippers of idols were put to shame and those who put their trust in graven images were confounded. In many
30 parts of that land the host of unbelievers were silenced, not daring to murmur, and all iniquity stopped her mouth.

The king rejoiced beyond belief to see the dearest fruits
33 of his labours now come to pass. But the unwearied preacher of the Gospel never ceased, now to persuade the obstinate,

now to instruct the ignorant, now to strengthen those frail
in the faith. In his reign he showed nothing of kingly pride,
nothing of tyranny, but rather furnished to all an example   3
of great humility and mildness. Concerned moreover for
the future welfare of the people he ruled, lest the lordly and
powerful should oppress the lowly with their might, he   6
composed and proclaimed laws both ecclesiastical and civil,
full of great wisdom and framed with wonderful discern-
ment. In them he assigned to each estate its proper rights, and   9
determined within strict bounds what authority the bishops
should have over their people and what deference the people
should show their bishops. In this he was a most moderate   12
and just judge, and wisely bearing in mind how often kings
arrogantly misused their subjects, he restrained and bridled
royal licence with the rigour of law. These laws reveal how   15
devoted this glorious king was to God, how benevolent to
his fellow-men.

Words cannot express the many benefits the oft-named   18
king conferred upon his people, the good he did while he
governed them, by enacting laws and relieving the poor,
by diligent preaching and by the example of his most holy   21
life. But in return he had many trials and tribulations to
endure from the people, until at length he could not oppose the multitude of evils. Thinking the moment required   24
it, he withdrew into Russia till the Lord should deign to
find a time suitable for him to fulfil his desire and purpose.
Let no one suppose that this most stalwart and steadfast   27
champion of Christ was subject to human weakness, that
he retreated for fear of martyrdom. For he had often courted
martyrdom of his own free will, as the outcome of events   30
and his illustrious death made manifest. For the benefit of
others he saved himself to await a more favourable moment,
when he might present more plentiful fruits to the Lord   33
and return with manifold interest the talent entrusted to him.

Therefore the glorious martyr of Christ went into Russia where he was nobly received by Jaroslav, the magnificent king of that realm, and held in the highest esteem as long as he chose to remain. He stayed there for some time, and left the inhabitants with a model of upright life and a famous recollection of his piety, charity, kindness and patience. At length, refined by the fire of persecution and exile, found acceptable and worthy to sustain greater trials, prompted by divine inspiration, he returned by way of Sweden to his native land. By the grace of God, conferred upon him more abundantly than ever, he was there received by many with ardent longing. Favoured and long wished for by good men, he appeared fearsome and terrible to opponents of wholesome instruction. Clad in the breastplate of faith, girded with the sword of the spirit which is the word of God, in honour and dishonour, evil report and good report, with the armour of righteousness on the right hand and the left, the illustrious preacher steadfastly sowed the word of faith wherever he went, ready to suffer any persecution for Christ's sake. He willingly put himself in the way of dangers, not refusing to accept martyrdom if it was God's will.

And since the labourer is worthy of his hire, it pleased the Lord at last to bring his champion out of the prison of the flesh, that he might receive in fullest and superabundant measure the reward of his labours and that the king might see the King in his beauty. People in that particular part of the country where his most holy body now rests were obdurate and inflexible in their malice, inexorable enemies of the truth and so of the king. The martyr of Christ chanced to come into that district to preach God's grace to the unbelieving people. When the enemies of the truth learnt this, they summoned a wicked council and gathered together against the Lord and his anointed. For his preaching of salvation was entirely opposed to them and their works.

Some of them were corrupted by the bribes of his enemy, a certain Knútr; some were prompted by malice alone and, further, were unwilling to receive a new religion, contrary to their ancestral laws. So they assembled an army and gave battle to the king at the place now called Stiklarstaðir, catching him unawares and at some little distance from his own men. But the most illustrious martyr was unafraid in the face of the multitude, his thoughts wholly centred on things celestial and in his innermost being desirous of attaining heaven through the crown of martyrdom. The warfare was at hand which he, the lover of peace, undertook to fight for the sake of justice and equity. He mustered his forces therefore, as well as he could in a short time, and went to meet his enemies.

Thereupon the Lord resolved to grant to his martyr the reward for which he had endured so many trials and to reveal to him his glory for which he had so long and eagerly thirsted. So in order to crown him with greater glory, God permitted the glorious martyr to fall by the spears of the wicked. He died in defence of the faith, cruelly cut off by enemies of the faith, four days before the first of August, on a Wednesday, in the year one thousand and twenty-eight after the Lord's incarnation. He went joyously from a soldier's camp to the King's eternal palace, from battle to the peace of God which passeth all understanding and to the praise and glory of our Lord, Jesus Christ, to whom is honour and glory for ever and ever. Amen.

Here ends the life of Saint Óláfr, king and martyr

Here his miracles begin

It is fitting to make brief mention of the many miracles
3 that the Lord has deigned to perform in order to make manifest
the merits of the glorious martyr Óláfr, so that the souls
of those who hear may be moved to praise and venerate
6 the divine mercy, and that it may be revealed to the faithful
what great grace and glory the Lord has bestowed upon
his saint.

9   Indeed, on the eve of the day when the illustrious Óláfr
suffered martyrdom, the Lord Jesus appeared to him, soothing
him with fair words, with words of solace. 'Come to me,'
12 he said, 'my beloved. It is time for you to reap the most
sweet fruits of your labours, and receive the crown of everlasting honour, enjoying communion with us in eternal
15 bliss.' The martyr, fully heartened by this vision, and elated
beyond measure by the ineffable delight he had received,
offered himself joyously to martyrdom, for now, by divine
18 inspiration, he understood the significance of the ladder,
raised up to the heavens, that he had seen in his dreams
not long before. By means of this ladder he was to ascend
21 happily to the sweetness that he had tasted.

Accordingly, when the time of his martyrdom had passed
and the royal attendants had washed his most holy body in
24 a certain house, the water, mixed with the blood that had
flowed from the wounds of the blessed martyr, was thrown
out through the door of the house. Now a certain blind man,
27 passing by the same house, fell down in a place that was
still wet with the bloodstained water. And when he put his
fingers, wet with that water, to his eyes again, at once the
30 darkness was cleared away, and he regained his former
sight.

He was greatly astonished, this man on whom the divine
33 marvel was accomplished, and seeking to discover whose
blood the water had been mixed with, he learned for certain

that he had recovered his sight through the powers of the
blessed Óláfr. All those who heard the news of the miracle
were awe-stricken, and with fitting proclamations they ex- 3
alted the Divine Mercy, who had deigned to glorify his
martyr with such an illustrious miracle.

How a certain chieftain of Ireland overcame, through 6
the intervention of the blessed Óláfr, a king who
unjustly opposed him

There was in Ireland a certain chieftain, Guthormr by name, 9
by birth a Norwegian, in fact a nephew of the blessed martyr Óláfr and a man distinguished in descent and mighty
in battle. He was allied and united in close fellowship with 12
Margaðr, the king of Dublin. Now it came to pass that the
two set out together on a raid, with a vast fleet, and returned enriched with many treasures and abundant booty. 15
Then one day, when they met to divide the spoils between
them, the aforesaid king, seeing the immeasurable plunder, was blinded by the love of avarice and, heedless of 18
their mutual alliance and reciprocal oath, he demanded that
the chieftain choose which one of two things he would have:
'Either,' he said, 'you will yield all the spoils to me, along 21
with the ships, or you will have an attack from me to suffer.'
Placed in these straits, the chieftain Guthormr did not know
where to turn. To yield the plunder along with the ships 24
seemed to him shameful and disgraceful beyond measure,
to go into battle would be highly dangerous. There was
indeed a great difference between the two armies, for the 27
king is said to have had fifteen ships, but the chieftain only
five. The troubled chieftain therefore sought a truce of two
days, that he might try to turn the tyrant from his evil purpose. 30
For that was the vigil of the feast of the blessed martyr
Óláfr. But because he could by no entreaties mollify the
spirit of the brute, he chose to die nobly rather than to bring 33

such shame and dishonour upon his kindred as to yield his
spoils and ships to the tyrant. And since no mortal aid was
3 to be had, he besought divine aid, and devoutly prayed the
blessed martyr Óláfr to succour him. He promised that he
would have a silver cross made for the church of the martyr,
6 if he delivered him from the hand of the treacherous king.
Why make many words of it? Having arrayed his forces,
he attacked the enemy lines and, fighting most mightily,
9 he overthrew the entire horde of savages, with the aid of
Christ and the intervention of the most glorious martyr.
Having thus gained an unexpected victory, and having
12 returned with a multitude of spoils and great rejoicing, he
had a silver cross made of unheard-of size. It exceeded in
length the measure of a human body, and he placed it in
15 the church of the blessed martyr, by his body, as a memorial
offering for the divine triumph and the unexpected victory
that he had won through Óláfr's holy merits.
18   Far and wide resounded the exalted fame of the illustrious martyr and the miracles that the Lord deigned to perform in order to proclaim his glory. Not content to be con-
21 fined to the boundaries of Norway, it spread to the ends of
the earth. In the royal city of Constantinople his memory
is renowned, and in that city a church has been built in
24 honour of the martyr. For it befell at one time that the emperor
of the aforesaid city, having assembled his army, went forth
to do battle against a certain king of the heathens. The armies
27 on both sides being arrayed for warfare and positioned with
martial skill, they entered into combat. The foreigners fell
upon the Christians most fiercely, and in the first encoun-
30 ter they were the victors. The greater part of the Greeks
fell and the might of the Christian army was enfeebled. A
small force remained which expected nothing but death.
33 The emperor, stricken and well-nigh heartbroken, turned
to divine aid, and with many tears they all together im-

plored the help of the blessed martyr, who they knew by
report often came to the aid of those fighting for righteousness. They vowed that they would build a church in   3
the royal city, in the name of the martyr and in honour of
the blessed Virgin Mary, if, by Óláfr's intervention, they
should return as victors. O glorious and extraordinary   6
miracle! The martyr appeared to some of the soldiers and
preceded the vanguard of the Christians as an illustrious
standard-bearer. Dread seized the enemy army, and they   9
all turned to flee, smitten with divine terror. Defended by
the aid of the martyr, a force by no means large harried
those fierce savages, although a great and powerful army, 12
not long before, had been unable to withstand them. Ines-
timable slaughter was made of the pagans, and the Christian victors returned with great spoils. Having returned to 15
Constantinople victorious, and mindful of the vow to the
blessed martyr, by which they had bound themselves, the
emperor therefore built a church in honour of the blessed 18
Virgin Mary, and the people's offering to the fabric-fund
was so devout and eager that, when an immense church had
been completed and everything necessary for its adornment 21
had been done, a great deal of the money that had been
offered was still left over. And by the splendour of the many
precious things that were sent from Constantinople, the 24
church in which Saint Óláfr rests bears witness that the
hearts of all were devoted to the service of the blessed martyr,
because of these and many other extraordinary acts of grace. 27

Concerning the loaves changed into stones in the oven

There was in Denmark a certain official, a man hateful and
vile, and, as is read of the unjust judge, he 'feared not God, 30
and neither regarded man.' This man had a serving-woman
who was born in the district of the blessed martyr Óláfr,
and she was most devoted to the veneration of the saint. 33

The official, being a malicious and wicked man, and one who took delight in deriding the praises of good men, did not believe the things that were said of the martyr. But whatever the common word of all men reported concerning his miracles and his glory, he deemed to be false and foolish rumour. Now it happened that the anniversary of the martyrdom of this same king and martyr came around, a day which the men of that region observe with great reverence. This worst of men, therefore, finding it a time meet to display his malice, showed openly by his deeds the depravity that he had long practised in his heart. For not only did he not wish to show respect to the saint's day, but in contempt of it, he even ordered the aforesaid woman, whom he knew to be more devoted than others to the veneration of the martyr, to take loaves to be baked on that festal day. Since she knew the perversity of the man and that she would suffer the severest punishments if she did not yield to his evil command, she obeyed, though unwillingly, the sacrilegious order. Much aggrieved, she took the loaves to the oven, importuning the saint with copious lamentations. She also declared and confirmed by oath that she would never again do honour to the martyr, unless he showed his power by definite signs in such a desperate situation. O new and hitherto unknown miracle! At one and the same moment, the most worthless of men was stricken with blindness, and the loaves that had been placed in the oven were changed to stones. One of those stones is preserved to this day in the church of the blessed martyr as proof and memorial of the miracle.

Concerning a boy's tongue that had been cut out and was restored to him at the sepulchre of the martyr

A certain boy having been falsely accused of a crime—as often the just bear the blame for the wicked—his tongue was cut out. Roused by the report of the miracles which, as he had often heard, were performed through the saint's holy merits, he went to the shrine of the martyr. With many tears he implored the saint, praying with loud lamentations that by his intervention he would restore to him the power of speech that he had unjustly lost. He had thus remained steadfastly at the tomb of the martyr for some time, in prayer and in tears, when at the time when he usually lapsed into peaceful slumber, he fell asleep. And behold, he saw coming forth from the shrine a man of middle height, with a handsome countenance, who, approaching nearer and opening the youth's mouth with his hand, drew forth the remaining part of his maimed tongue and stretched it out with such force that the youth, unable to bear the violence of the effort, was compelled to cry out in his sleep. And thus arising from sleep healed, he broke forth, rejoicing, into praises of God and the martyr. And thus it was that he who had come to the tomb of the saint mourning and mute returned joyfully to his home, able to speak freely.

A certain other man had been taken prisoner by the Slavs, who cut out his tongue. By chance he escaped. Coming to the shrine of the martyr and praying with heartfelt misery that his tongue might be restored to its former wholeness, he recovered the power of speech which he had lost, and in that church he dedicated his life to perpetual service of the martyr.

A certain woman, who was so bent by deformity that her feet pressed back against her thighs, was conveyed to the tomb of the martyr. When she had kept vigil there for a very long time in tears and supplication, she was restored to complete health. With sinews lengthened, legs straightened and feet strengthened, with the use and proper form of each limb restored, she walked back to her home, lighthearted and rejoicing.

Concerning a priest whose eyes, tongue and legs were maimed, and who was restored to health through the powers of the martyr

There were two brothers of noble family, who possessed an abundance of worldly wealth. They had a sister, who was outwardly comely but most careless regarding the slanders of the wicked, as the consequences proved. Being closely acquainted with a certain English priest who lived in her brothers' house, this woman conferred many a kindness upon him, with sincere piety. It happened nonetheless that injurious suspicion arose concerning her. But since malicious rumour easily corrupts the minds of those who listen to it, relentless talk caused blame to be laid upon the innocent priest. Now because of her great familiarity with the priest, her brothers were as certain of the matter as if it had been proved. Outraged beyond measure and incensed with boundless wrath, they concealed their fury with dissembling. Indeed, on a certain day they summoned the priest, who suspected no evil, to go with them, supposedly to attend to some business, and they took along a certain man of theirs who was privy to the wickedness they had planned. When therefore they reached a more secluded place, far distant from their home, they seized the priest, who had feared nothing of the sort, and broke his legs, cut out his tongue, and gouged the eyes from his head. Finally, when they saw him painfully trying to speak by moving the stump of his tongue, they fell upon him, pulled out with pincers the part of his tongue that they had left him, and cut it again. Then, left there half-dead, he was taken by a certain poor woman to her house. But he who had experienced such cruelty from men did not despair of the mercy of heaven. His mouth being silent, his devout heart spoke the more tellingly; being weaker, he was stronger and mightier in faith, and having turned wholeheartedly to the glorious martyr Óláfr, of whose powers he had heard such great things, he begged him not to fail him in such need, pleading all the more piteously as he was the more pitiable, and the more desperately, the greater was his despair. Thus, persevering in prayer and lamentation and with a crushed heart, he implored the aid of the martyr without cease, a pitiful wretch deserving of pity. At last, on the following day, he was eased by the serenity of sleep. And behold, the holy martyr appeared to him, saying that he was Óláfr, whom he had invoked so devoutly and urgently. Then, after touching with a gentle hand the priest's eyes and legs and other injured places, finally, putting his hand to his tongue, he pulled at the root of the tongue with such force that the priest gave a loud cry, compelled by exceedingly great pain. After the healing touch of the martyr, he who had suffered such grave wounds was at once so succoured by the plenitude of divine mercy that it seemed as if nothing at all had happened to him. His tongue was renewed; his legs were healed; his eyes were restored; and his wounds and injuries of all sorts were completely cured. However, to bear witness that his eyes had been torn out, a white scar remained on his eyelids.

How he burned in his palm the shavings of a stick that he had been cutting on a Sunday

Let us proceed to that miracle which is on every tongue, one that, although we introduce it later in the narrative, was nevertheless the first of all that we relate, as far as the order of events is concerned. For it came to pass while the saint was still living in the flesh, that on a certain Sunday the glorious king Óláfr had chanced upon a stick where he was sitting, and he was whittling it with a small knife that he had in his hand, forgetful that it was the Lord's Day. For they observe holy days with great strictness in Norway, nor does anyone venture to do any work then, great

or small. Therefore, one of the king's attendants, seeing that the king was carving on the Sabbath, but not daring
3 to say outright that it was Sunday, reminded him with these words: 'Lord king', he said, 'tomorrow will be Monday.' By this admonition the king was recalled to himself, and
6 earnestly sorry that he had been cutting a stick on Sunday, he gathered all the shavings of the stick on his hand, set fire to them, and burned them. And when they had been burned,
9 his hand was seen to be uninjured. Thus was repeated the miracle of the three boys that was once acclaimed in Babylon. The fire had its natural power to consume the bits of stick,
12 yet it was not at all able to harm the hand of the blameless king.

How a certain peasant escaped hanging by calling upon
15   *the blessed Óláfr*

Likewise at a certain time there occurred another illustrious and unheard-of miracle. For a certain peasant, a frank and
18 blameless man, was wrongly charged with the crime of theft by certain powerful men of his district, who were moved not by justice but by malice. And without an inquiry he
21 was tried, protesting his innocence, and through the iniquity of his enemies he was sentenced to be hanged. And when, despite his pleas, the tormented and wretched man saw no
24 recourse to justice in a perverse people, he despaired altogether of mortal aid. So in his heart he looked only to the mercy of God, and earnestly prayed to the blessed martyr
27 Óláfr that he, who often by his prayers mercifully delivered the guilty from their just deserts, should for justice sake succour through prayer one who was innocent in the
30 sight of God. Why make many words of it? Their iniquity came forth from a gross heart; without delay it was put into effect. One who was guiltless was hanged by those
33 who deserved to be hanged. A true lawgiver, Saint Óláfr

had pity upon the pitiful wretch and came to the aid of the one who called upon him, asking for justice by virtue of his innocence. For as soon as he was raised from the ground, he saw, as if in a vision, the holy martyr Óláfr place a plank beneath his feet, and by its support he remained unharmed for nearly nine hours, until his wife and his sons returned, having obtained permission from a certain nobleman to take down his body and commit it to the tomb. And when they came to take him away, his son climbed the tree from which he hung suspended, a tree rooted in a certain high precipice. When the aforesaid youth had inched his way to the top, with a vigorous stroke he cut through the rope that held him up. When this had been done, his hapless body had such a steep fall that it seemed he must be dashed to pieces; no one would have thought that he could possibly be still alive and well. But neither the severity of the fall nor the height of the crag could inflict harm upon one to whom, for justice sake, the power of the martyr had extended aid. He remained as one fast asleep, recalling the vision as if in a dream. When the coldness passed from his limbs, however, their strength increased, and, having regained his senses, he gradually recovered. He went in haste to the holy martyr's shrine, and to God's glory revealed to the archbishop there and to the clergy in turn what had befallen him, which was confirmed by the testimony of many.

Concerning the audacity of a certain man and the punishment of his audacity

It happened at one time that a dangerous fire burned the city in which the holy martyr rests, and to protect the church the martyr's body was therefore placed before the flames as a defence. But a certain man, who was quite rash, approached and began to beat the shrine of the martyr, threatening that all would be left to burn if he did not manifest his customary

aid and safeguard with his prayers the church and the still
undamaged buildings. The church, indeed, remained un-
3 touched, but that cleric was seized on the following night
with a severe pain in the eyes. He recovered his health at
last in that very church, through the prayers of the holy
6 martyr.

Concerning a youth delivered from captivity by the
intercession of the martyr

9 A certain youth, Danish by birth, was taken captive by Slavs
and held with other prisoners in the strictest confinement.
For during the day he remained in chains, without a guard,
12 but at night the son of his keeper was chained to him
with a fetter on one leg so as to guard him closely. But
this wretched man, lying awake in his anguish, fearfully
15 deliberated what course of action remained to him. He feared
hard labour; he was in terror of tortures; and because he
despaired of ransom, he endured the depths of misery. Since
18 he had in fact been redeemed from captivity by his relations
twice before, they would find it both difficult and costly
to do so again. Oh how grievous is life when death is longed
21 for, how utterly wretched it is to live when death seems to
hold sway over life! Hence he was thrown into doubt, whether
death should put a swift end to his present suffering, or
24 whether he might have better fortune if he lived. He killed
the son of his captor and cut off his foot; then, carrying
his chains, he fled to the woods. But at daybreak the deed
27 was discovered; a clamour was raised and the malefactor
was sought. Two dogs were loosed that had been remark-
ably well trained to track down Christian fugitives. Their
30 skill immediately showed the search-party the way, and
their barking betrayed the man's hiding-place. The wretch
was captured, dragged away, beaten with scourges, laid low,
33 nearly given over to death; he had no man's pity to help

him, nor any mercy from the heartless pagans. Indeed, only
the inborn villainy of the heathen prevented his impend-
ing death, for avarice overcame their natural hatred. That   3
most wretched vice so possessed his captor that the youth's
expected ransom outweighed the vengeance owed for his
son's blood. Thereupon he was dragged back and thrust   6
into prison with sixteen other Christians, and he was confined
more strictly than the others, with fetters of wood as well
as iron. His former suffering was but a shadow compared   9
to this, and his past woes seemed to him, without doubt,
merely foreshadowings of those to come. For no one who
approached him showed pity to the helpless man, but in-   12
deed each one inflicted torment on the wretch as if on a
condemned man. Nothing was given him, nothing was allowed, save that he might suffer all that unbridled cruelty   15
could inflict on him. And thus his misery grew so great
that those who were bound with the same chains lamented
his misery and counselled him therefore to dedicate him-   18
self by a vow to the holy martyr Óláfr, and if the saint
delivered him, to serve him always in his church. When he
had gladly accepted this advice and was sleeping that night   21
among his companions, he saw a man of middle height
standing near him and calmly addressing him with these
words: 'Why, O wretch,' he said, 'do you not rise?' And   24
he replied: 'My lord, who are you?' He responded: 'I am,'
he said, 'that Óláfr whom you have invoked.' And he said:
'Lord, I would willingly rise, but I am bound by one foot   27
with a shackle, and also chained in fetters with my companions.' But he said, 'Arise quickly, without fear, for you
are free.' At once, therefore, when he was awakened from   30
sleep, he related the dream to his companions, who at once
urged him to test whether what he had seen was true. And
straightway he was seen to get to his feet and he felt him-   33
self free of every chain. But some of his companions claimed

that this had been done for him in vain, since the door was fortified most securely with bolts and bars on the outside.

3 A certain old man, however, who was held in the same confinement, admonished him not to doubt the aid of the martyr, by whose manifest favour he was now free. 'Do
6 not believe,' he said, 'that such a famous miracle has been performed in vain, as if such a glorious act, failing to achieve its due success, should show itself more worthy of silence
9 than of praise, as if, that is to say, suffering should come of the martyr's aid rather than freedom. Bestir yourself, therefore, and feel the door, because if you get out you
12 will be sure of safety.' It happened in just that way, for he found the door open and fled to the woods again. Why delay this tale? As soon as they discovered this, they searched
15 as before, having loosed the dogs. The wretched man lay still and saw them coming. But the men's eyesight was clouded and the dogs' sense of smell lost its natural keenness, and
18 so they passed by where he lay and at last returned home, as much bewildered as disappointed by what had occurred. But the glory of the works of the blessed martyr grew even greater;
21 for, having raised this man from the depths of affliction, he by no means allowed him to incur further danger when he had reached the seashore. For it would not avail him to
24 be delivered from tortures into complete safety, unless his deliverance also afforded him healing. His head had been struck so hard in the cruel beating that he had entirely lost
27 his hearing. Freed, therefore, in the aforesaid way, and having been joined by two Christians who were worn by long captivity, he embarked on the dangers of the sea; with speedy
30 decision he cast aside sloth, and—to put the matter briefly—made his escape, together with his companions. And so, when he came to the church of the blessed martyr to give
33 thanks for the help he had received, he rejoiced in the recovery of perfect health. Having been granted his wish,

however, he soon began to change his mind about fulfilling his vow, until, now that he was hale and hearty, he took flight, his resolution overthrown. And when after a day's journey he had been hospitably received, for charity's sake, by a certain venerable man, he saw by night three maidens standing near him, fair of face and clad in radiant attire. They severely reprimanded him, and asked how it was that he did not fear to offend the saint by his rash venture, after having seen so many of his powerful miracles, and how he dared to withdraw from the service he had promised in return and confirmed on oath. And so, having been awakened by this vision, when he arose in the morning he related to his host everything that had happened to him from the beginning, and by his advice he was urged to return at once. These miracles are proclaimed by a manifest sign, since we have seen (glory be to the Saviour!) the aforesaid youth in the church of the blessed martyr, dedicated to his service for life, and we have had sight of the marks of the fetters upon his limbs.

Concerning a woman delivered from the disease of epilepsy

In that city which now possesses the precious shrine of the relics of the blessed martyr Óláfr there was a certain woman who had long been oppressed by the affliction of the disease of epilepsy, and she was given in marriage to a certain youth, who was ignorant of her ailment. All things having been solemnised, therefore, that by custom the nuptial rite required, as they lay sleeping on a certain night her infirmity returned, and her wits left her as she was thrown about, frothing at the mouth; her body, moreover, was dreadfully deformed and altered in colour, as if bereft of life. When her husband saw this, he said that he was the most unfortunate of men, since for his sins it had fallen to his

lot to be joined so indissolubly to such an irremediable
evil. Nevertheless, he asked how it had come to pass, and
3 whether she had ever sought any remedy. And she confessed that she was tormented in this way nearly every month,
and that no physician had bestowed his skill upon her. The
6 woman was racked as much by compassion for her husband as by her own infirmity, for his grief was revealed
all the while by the expression of his face. Placed in these
9 straits, she importuned with constant prayer the glorious
Virgin, who is indeed the Mother of Mercy, and the holy
martyr Óláfr, that he would by his power give her relief
12 and put an end to her sorrows. And so, having gone to her
priest, she confessed those sins which the frailty of the
flesh had prompted, but also explained the causes of her
15 suffering and sought his counsel concerning a remedy. But
he, guided to the gospel by divine impulse, quoted from
the holy words, 'This kind of disease goeth not out but by
18 prayer and fasting.' Exhorted by these words, she and her
husband then, along with others inflicted by various infir-
mities, went to the church of the blessed martyr. Having
21 brought plenty of lamps, on the night held sacred to him
they held vigil with complete devotion and fasting, for the
feast-day dedicated to the martyr was on the morrow. And
24 so, when the clergy had observed the nocturnal office proper
for the celebration of the day when the glorious champion
of Christ received the crown of martyrdom, she returned
27 home and in due course received perfect health. For, although
the severity of the malady was such that from youth up-
ward she was tormented every month without exception,
30 yet after receiving this grace she has never since suffered
an attack at any time. Afterwards, because of the help they
had received, their devotion grew so great that every year
33 on the eve of the feast of Saint Óláfr, the same night on
which she rejoiced in her recovered health, they have served

God most zealously, strictly fasting, with vigil and with alms.

How a fire was extinguished when his image was set   3
against it

In a certain city in Russia, called Hólmgarðr, it happened that such a fire suddenly blazed up that the destruction of   6 the whole township seemed at hand. The townspeople, utterly undone by fear, thronged to a certain priest of the Roman dispensation, Stephanus by name, who then served in the   9 church of Saint Óláfr, so that they might try the powers of the blessed martyr in such a crisis, and so that the reports of him that they had heard from rumour might be proved   12 by definite signs. Now the priest, by no means a laggard, thought well of their purpose, seized the saint's image and with his own arms set it before the flames; but the fire passed   15 no farther, and the part of the city that remained was saved from the conflagration.

What happened in a certain district called Þelamǫrk is also   18 worth the telling. For on a certain day the inhabitants of that district held a great gathering to discuss the construction of a church in honour of the blessed martyr, and because   21 they had not found stones that could be used for the purpose, they determined instead upon a building of wood. The man who had been brought in as master-mason of the   24 proposed work, having been frustrated several times, set out upon his return journey, but on that very day, through a divine miracle, the slopes of a neighbouring mountain   27 were shattered with astounding force. Afterwards, they collected enough stones there that were suitable for the work, and they most devoutly undertook the labour of build-   30 ing the church.

Likewise in that district, in a neighbouring town, it befell that a little boy wandered away from his family, who   33 were at a meal with friends, and they besought their help to look for him. When they had scoured the entire town and not found the child at all, they did not abandon the effort but searched again on the next day. And when the exhausted searchers had found no trace of him, they returned, consoling each other. Having made an invocation to Saint Óláfr, they took up a collection, each according to his means, and sent it to the church of the holy martyr. Then, under the saint's patronage, they made a third attempt to find the boy. And as soon as they set out, they found him sleeping in a certain place near the house, where they had certainly searched with care before. They returned home gladdened, and for the return of one whom they had mourned as lost they praised the great works of the Lord, who has deigned to perform so many miracles for his champion.

Concerning a youth delivered from the power of the Devil

We have briefly touched upon certain works which the Lord has performed for his martyr's sake, but not the least among the rest is a miracle which still moves the hearts of the faithful. For just as the soul of any believer is superior by nature to the body, so is the death of the soul deemed to be more grievous and its salvation more precious. For truly what the Enemy of humankind did in Paradise, he does not desist from doing every day among us. For he strives to tear out the righteousness from the heart of every person and to insinuate the false charms of his promises. For he makes light of God's admonitions and urges belief in what he falsely promises; he offers mere worldly honours, and makes light of the eternal punishments of which God warns us. Our first parent was deceived by this bane of pride, through which his unwary descendants are wounded every day by

the Enemy. He made use of this dart when he so corrupted
a certain youth by the venom of his wicked temptation that,
heedless of the Creator's command, he was enticed to fol- 3
low the spirit of pride. This unfortunate wretch was from
the district which is called Ytterøya, and the ancient Enemy
had stricken him with such blindness that the torments to 6
come held no terrors for him, such was his desire for the
goods of this world. Indeed, in the hope of fleeting honour, he fell under the sway of eternal death, and he became 9
a slave and sacrifice to the Devil when, through apostasy,
he denied his Creator and lost the freedom of the children
of God. And when by evil instigation he was drawn head- 12
long into every sin, and the Enemy exulted as if sure of
his prey, then came the feast day of the blessed martyr.
And when the crowds, as usual, had flocked to his church, 15
this youth was also in attendance, that he might be drawn
the more to guilty worldly desires by the unbridled wan-
tonness of forbidden sights, and that he might be bound 18
the more to the Enemy, the more he fell by yielding to his
temptation. But truly the Lord, who desires the salvation
of all, pitied his dying sheep the more, the worse he knew 21
him to be deceived. For, when the glorious body of the
blessed martyr Óláfr was borne in procession from the church,
the aforesaid youth began to weigh within himself the glory 24
of the martyr, and to consider in his heart his own wretched
state. He reflected upon the glory he had lost, and brooded
fearfully over the terrors of damnation he had incurred. 27
For truly such grace had touched his spirit from the salutary presence of the martyr that the veil of sin had been lifted, and his humbled and grieving spirit showed outwardly, 30
with tears of contrition, what he suffered inwardly from
guilt. And when the bier was lifted from the place where
it stood and carried away, he betook himself to the same 33
place where he had seen that the martyr's body rested. And

there, with a downcast spirit, he began to beseech the holy
martyr with great lamentation that he might be found worthy
3 to be freed by the saint's prayers from the chain of damnation that bound him. And thus, the prayers of the martyr having been heard, he was roused as if from the ob-
6 livion of death and recovering little by little his lost strength
of mind, he discovered in his humility what he had lost in
his pride. But he dreaded to open the wound of his un-
9 chaste heart, and confounded by shame he hesitated to avail
himself of the remedy of confession. Truly he had need of
the martyr's help to rescue him from the mire that held him
12 fast, lest the deep pit of vice should swallow once more the
unwary captive whom the mercy of the martyr had released
from the jaws of hell. And so by divine providence he was
15 seized by a most grievous weakness, nor did he recover
from it until he had disclosed his sin in confession, and
washed away the wrath of the Creator with worthy pen-
18 ance. But when his soul had been saved, without delay the
joyous youth regained his bodily powers, so that the illness of the body might teach how his soul had been en-
21 chained. Without doubt, the cure arose whence the illness
had first come. For as his body was stricken helpless by
the chain of the soul, so did its salvation depend upon the
24 loosing of that chain, and he uplifted himself all the more
devoutly to do good afterwards, because he knew that he
had been cast down the more vilely before.

27   *Concerning two blind persons and a mute who were
restored to health on Saint Óláfr's day*

Now, in the year when the church of the blessed martyr
30 Óláfr was newly invested with archiepiscopal honour and the
pallium, crowded throngs of people gathered there, among
them three invalids who had come from a great distance,
33 suffering from afflictions. Together they had come to the

church of the blessed martyr, hoping through his patronage to achieve the benefit of health, especially on that very day when the martyr won joy everlasting, casting off for Christ's sake the bonds of the flesh. There was indeed among them a certain blind man who was found worthy, on the eve of Saint Óláfr's day, to be comforted by the joy of sight. Further, on the following day, when the rites of the procession were solemnised, and the bier had been set down in the churchyard as usual, a certain dumb man received the grace of speech, and rejoicing he loosed the long hindered powers of his tongue in praises of the Saviour. In addition to these, there was a certain woman from the distant parts of Sweden who had chosen to travel to the abode of the holy martyr to pray there. Although she suffered many difficulties on the way, as much from her blindness as from the hardships of travelling, nevertheless, firm in faith and strengthened by hope, she completed the journey she had undertaken. And when she entered his glorious church on his feast-day, and the most holy offices of mass were being celebrated, she was found worthy to receive the longed-for joy of sight which she had been without for a full thirteen years.

Concerning the healing of a certain mute

A certain Varangian had bought a slave in Russia, a youth of good character, but dumb. Since he could say nothing about himself, who his people might be was unknown, but the skill in which he was trained showed that he had lived among the Varangians, for he knew how to make the weapons that they alone employ. A long while after he was sold, when he had known various masters, he was finally bought by a merchant who out of regard for his piety released him from the yoke of slavery. Having gained his longed-for freedom, he went to the city called Hólmgarðr, and stayed for a few

days in the home of a certain pious matron who had received him for hospitality's sake. Now this woman was
3 zealous in devotion to the blessed martyr Óláfr, and she
applied herself to prayer in his church at all hours. Thus it
was that during the night-time she seemed to see the bles-
6 sed martyr Óláfr, bidding her to bring the aforesaid boy with
her to the church, and hastening to obey, she straightway
brought him to the morning service. Then when they came
9 to the church together, the boy soon fell asleep, and the
man who had first appeared to the woman, ordering that
the youth be brought to the church to be healed—for his
12 features and apparel presently showed that it was he—now
appeared to the boy and bestowed a cure upon him by the
favour of divine grace.

15   *Concerning the healing of the king of Norway*

A long time after the elevation of the martyr, a church was
built in his honour in the place where, through the shed-
18 ding of his blood, he had taken the shorter way to life's
reward. Now, at the time when the bishop came to dedicate
the church, it happened that the king fell gravely ill in that
21 neighbourhood. For his knee was so grievously afflicted with
an abscess that his whole thigh and shin were constantly
rigid with an unbearable swelling. Urged by his piety to at-
24 tend the dedication, and with his infirmity growing worse,
he was carried to a ship and brought by river to a place
near the church. Then, conducted in a litter by his attend-
27 ants, he was set down in the church. When the ceremony had
been completed with the customary solemnity, the king's
attention was drawn to the stone upon which the blessed
30 martyr had fallen in death, which still shows the stain of
his blood. The topmost part of this stone protruded from
the altar, and the king then approached and laid his knee
33 and the other afflicted parts of his leg near to it. Without

delay, the richness of divine mercy straightway afforded such aid that the swelling was allayed that very evening and, now that his pain had been removed, he was found able to perform any duties, with all his limbs as agile as if he had never been stricken.

Concerning two girls who were freed from a contraction of the limbs

Furthermore, at that same time a certain little girl, who had been bent and deformed since infancy, came out of the church healed. Likewise, a year later, on Saint Óláfr's day, another girl won the bounty of the like grace, for her sinews were withered, and for more than five years her heels had been joined to her haunches. With the assistance of the faithful, she was carried before the door of the choir, and when the saint's most holy body was lifted for the procession, a cracking of stretching sinews was heard, and at that moment she was healed by a miraculous power.

In the same year, in the place called Stiklarstaðir, a certain woman recovered her sight at the shrine of the blessed martyr. In childhood the pupil of her eye had been injured by another child with the point of a small knife, and the damage to one eye had caused both to be afflicted with blindness, but when her blindness had been cleared away by the intervention of the martyr she rejoiced in the recovery of her former sight.

Concerning a merchant healed of a broken leg

On the eighth day after Epiphany, a certain merchant who was wintering in Iceland fell down on the ice and broke his leg in three places, a break which, for ten weeks, no skill was able to mend. Indeed, on Palm Sunday, seeing that his leg was now livid and wasting away, he lamented greatly and implored with many sighs the intercession of

the blessed Óláfr, vowing that he would visit his church within three years, and that he would always keep the eve
3 of Saint Óláfr by fasting on bread and water, if he should be cured through his patronage. Thereupon, he was overtaken by a peaceful sleep, and in the morning he was able
6 to move his foot and even to stand. Indeed, on the following Sunday, which was Easter, he went out with a firm stride.

Likewise there came two brothers from the French city cal-
9 led Chartres, one of whom was a cleric, the other a layman. These two, driven, truly, by a boundless rage because they had been deprived of their paternal inheritance, had killed
12 their mother and infant brother in a fire, along with the soldier who had married their mother and deprived them of their inheritance. In penance, therefore, they had been
15 bound with iron bands and exiled from their homeland. Performing their penance devoutly, they had gone as far as Jerusalem, and there, at the tomb of the Lord, the iron
18 that bound the arm of the layman broke apart. But since rest was not yet given after toil, they traversed nearly all the Christian world for the sake of absolution. And so they
21 came to the church of the blessed Óláfr; before the altar, on the third Sunday of Lent, the aforesaid brother was set free from the remaining iron, which was still bound around
24 his loins when he arrived.

How the barn of a certain peasant was saved,
undamaged, from a neighbouring fire

27 Henceforth, although the prolix narrative may seem tedious at times and the unpolished diction may weigh upon the listener, nevertheless, trusting to the devotion of your
30 piety we shall undertake to make known to your charity, in a few words, some of those things that we know have been done in recent times. Thus, in the district called Mœrr,
33 not far from the church of the blessed Óláfr, a certain peasant

had loaded the year's produce into his barn, the walls of which were constructed of leafy branches. But because the narrowness of the barn could not hold the abundance of the harvest, he had put the remaining crop in a heap beside the wall of the barn, so close that there was hardly a cubit's distance in between. It happened, however, that the crop in neighbouring barns was suddenly consumed by a fire, and the blaze was spread wildly by blowing winds to the walls woven of dry branches. The man, seeing this, implored the succour of Saint Óláfr in this extremity, adding that if any of his property were saved from the fire, he would give over half of everything to the church of the blessed Óláfr. That said, the fire was driven back, without doing any harm either to the crop or to the walls of the barn. Moreover, what we relate to your charity, we have learned from the testimony of people from that neighbourhood, and it has been clearly confirmed by the donation of money that we have received.

In addition, one day when a tempest had arisen, a certain ship was driven against a headland where the rough coastline was like a wall, steep and unapproachable, offering access only to birds. The sailors, dumbfounded by the crashing of the sea and the height of the cliff, therefore importuned Saint Óláfr with heartfelt lamentations to hearken to them when death was so dreadfully near. But then the helpless ship was guided back against the fury of the storm, swifter by command than by the power of a thousand men, and on entering the welcome harbour, the sailors, mindful of the martyr's help, gladly contributed the aforesaid ship to us for the construction of his church.

Concerning two boys delivered from captivity

In the district called Angrar there was a certain man who was rich in property and not of the lowest lineage. He had three sons, the heirs of his wealth, the youngest of whom

had strayed among pagans and been taken captive. Indeed, although the pagans were as far divided from Christians
3 in distance as they were in faith, nevertheless, so frequent were the dealings between them for the redemption of prisoners that the pagans knew very well about the father's
6 riches, and so they set the ransom-fee at forty marks. When the old man heard that, he absolutely refused to hand over his goods to a pagan, whatever might become of the boy.
9 Sustained, therefore, by faith and with increasing hope, he turned to the blessed Óláfr for help, to whose service he was most faithfully devoted, along with his sons and his
12 whole household. Every year he took the responsibility for collecting the annual donation in the aforesaid district and sent it to the church of the blessed Óláfr. Wherefore, con-
15 fident in the powers of the martyr, he entrusted his son to him, promising a gold ring of great weight to his church, as if by way of tribute from his forebears, if by the saint's
18 help he might gain the longed-for return of the lost hostage. At the same time, while the boy was held in the custody of the pagans along with another Christian, he saw
21 in his dreams a certain man of middle height and with a handsome countenance, who stood there and questioned him about his rank and station. When he had made suit-
24 able replies to him the boy also asked the name of the one who appeared to him in this way. And he said, 'I am called Óláfr. I live in your district and often visit your father's
27 house. Because of this, I wish you to know that ransom has now been paid for you. Therefore, on the eve of Maundy Thursday, you will escape the enemy's domain and have
30 our safe-conduct to your own people.' Then when the boy awakened from sleep, he recalled the vision and related it to his fellow captive, and at the appointed time he kept
33 the saint's promise in mind. For on the night in question, when none of the pagans was awake, they escaped together,

laden with rattling chains and fettered with shackles. And because the encumbrance of the chains hindered them from going farther, they hid in a place near the buildings, lest they should be discovered by daylight. And when the morning came, the heathen people searched through every hiding-place. Shielded by divine protection, however, they were betrayed neither by the vigilance of the searchers nor by the noise of the chains when they tried to break them. And so, heartened by these signs, they were made more certain that they would reach refuge with the aid of divine mercy. So, having got rid of their chains, they crossed the pagan lands quickly, travelling only by night and seeking the nearest safe hiding-place every morning. Desire gave them unflagging strength without stint; fear of being recaptured took away their weariness, until, through the intervention of the martyr, the divine will restored them unharmed to their friends and fellows.

Likewise concerning two boys miraculously rescued from a waterfall through the powers of the blessed Óláfr

Also worthy of note is an event which happened recently, as we know from the statements of many, in a part of Europe beyond the southern mountains. While two boys were play-ing in a certain river, they got into a little boat that they happened to find, and it was silently carried by the currents toward a waterfall where the river made a dangerous drop over a steep cliff. Seeing that immediate death threatened them, the boys tearfully called upon Saint Óláfr with all their might, and at once, by God's mercy, they came to rest against a certain rock that jutted up in the middle of the river where the water rushed violently through a nar-rower curve, on the brink of the falls. The little boat went over the precipice, but the boys, clinging together, held fast to the aforesaid rock. Now the father of the boys had awaited

their return all night, unaware of what had happened to
them. In the morning he set out with his friends and neighbours to look for them at the riverbank where he had left
them playing. Then, when he saw them standing on the rock
and calling tearfully for their father, he suffered more cruelly than if they had been quickly carried off to their fate,
for their death would be painfully prolonged before his eyes,
instead of taking place at a distance. But because the inac-
cessibility of the place and the danger of the waterfall prevented human aid, those who had gathered commended the
souls of the boys to God, and returned home, exhausted by
toil and wakefulness. That night, when the father fell asleep
for a short while, there appeared a man with a pleasant
face, who, when asked his name, said that he was called
Óláfr. Holding out his arms with one athwart the other,
crosswise, he said, 'By a device fashioned in this wise, the
sons for whom you lament will be brought to shore. For,
mark, the man who will deliver them will soon be here.' Then
the father, recalling the vision, freely related it to everyone who came. And when a certain man arrived and heard
it, he said he was an artisan and undertook the work. When
the device was completed, it was thrust by the concerted
effort of many all the way out to the rock, forming a sort
of bridge over which the boys crawled until they reached
the welcome embraces of their kin. Then truly the father
and one of the boys hastened at once to the abode of the
blessed martyr to give thanks, and there they related all
that had happened to them, with the corroboration of neighbours.

How a certain deacon was delivered from a painful disease and from a sinful desire

A certain deacon, Danish by birth, came to the city of the
blessed Óláfr, and there he fell into the frailty of the flesh

and fathered many sons. As the number of his sons grew, so he was oppressed by greater poverty, and because of the neediness of his wards he came to his senses at last. Upon seeking our counsel, he admitted that he had been a monk, and, having received admonitions for his salvation, he promised to return to the monastic life. After a short time had passed, however, the spark of repentance that had been kindled was extinguished by baneful desire, and when he was held fast in the grip of his former lust, he was smitten, in divine punishment, with an unbearably painful swelling of his virile member. Unable to rest, therefore, and forced by the extreme pain to wander about, whenever he was allowed he threw himself down in his distress before the altar of the blessed Óláfr, although he was unworthy and a hardened sinner. Although impenitent all the while, he did not fear to prostrate himself there again and again, until at last he was overcome by sleep. And behold, a man came to him in the guise of a physician, and declaring, when asked his name, that he was Óláfr whom he had invoked, he pierced the sufferer's aching member with a hot iron. Now when the horror of the vision had awakened him, the organ that had been touched by the iron in his dream felt enveloped in fiery pain. Thereupon he sought a warm bath, so that the severity of the torment might at least be made more bearable by the balm of the soothing waters. While he was settled in it, his member, eased and unswollen, fell against his stomach where the iron had seemed to touch, and the power of sinning had left it. Moreover, what we have related to your charity about this matter, we have ascertained ourselves from the testimony of elders of our church.

There came two Spanish brothers from the region of Galicia who had killed their mother when she threw herself in the way of the swords with which they had attacked their step-father. Moreover, when the man fled and took

refuge in a monastery, they consigned it to the flames, burning him along with five monks. In consequence, bound with
3 iron and the most onerous penance, they made a pilgrimage throughout all the lands of the faithful. At last they were driven to these most remote parts, led by the fame of
6 the martyr. Before the altar of the blessed Óláfr the younger of the brothers, who seemed near to death from the swelling of his arm and the biting of the iron, was delivered from
9 both shackle and pain on a Sunday night during matins.

Likewise, during the following winter, a certain youth who had long been mute recovered his speech.
12 There was also in the vicinity of the city a certain peasant, Þórðr by name, called 'Inair' in Norwegian. He had a son who was much beloved, being an only child, but the
15 boy's knees were so bent that his feet seemed to be joined to his shanks. And because the father was grievously distressed by the child's suffering, he brought him to the church
18 of the blessed martyr on Saint Óláfr's eve. Now when the boy was lying asleep beside his father, he saw in his dreams a certain man who pulled his bent legs straight with such
21 force that the boy was compelled to cry out to him to be more gentle. But then, awakened from sleep, he rose up healed.
24 Likewise, in the district called Sogn, it happened that a building called a bath-house belonging to a certain peasant was consumed by such a violent fire that flames poured
27 forth from the upper vent as well as the door. When the peasant saw this, he was dismayed at the sudden catastrophe, and he dedicated a fifth part of his properties to the
30 blessed Óláfr if by his intervention he would deliver them from the fire. That done, he betook himself to the other buildings, to save his goods, but as he was doing so, he
33 wondered why the progress of the raging fire appeared to be slower than usual. He approached the door, opened it

and looked in, but he found that the fire was as fully extinguished as if the whole building had been drenched with
water. Without delay he summoned neighbours, had the   3
buildings valued and sent to us, at Bergen, the part of their
worth that belonged to the martyr.

At another time, during the reign of King Eysteinn, a   6
certain queen was suspected of having secretly carried off
the body of the martyr into Denmark. Therefore it seemed to
the king and to everyone else that an investigation of this   9
matter should be undertaken, and to this end they opened
up the shrine in which lay the most holy body of the saint.
When it was opened, such a sweet fragrance pervaded the   12
entire church that all those who partook of that experience
understood fully that they had savoured a heavenly, not
an earthly, sweetness.   15

A certain dumb man, who had by custom been receiving our charity for six years, recovered his speech on the
day of the resurrection of the Lord.   18

*An additional treatise by Bishop Eysteinn of Norway
concerning the miracles of the blessed Óláfr*

Having read all those accounts which antiquity has entrusted   21
to us concerning the life and miracles of the blessed Óláfr,
we deem it fitting that we, who have been personally en-
lightened by his widespread miracles in our own day, should   24
also commit to the attention of future generations, in writing, those things which have been performed by miraculous
powers, to his greater glory, as we have seen for ourselves   27
or have learnt from the testimony of truthful men. Truly,
as we are enjoined by the duty of charity to suffer with
those in affliction so doubtless are we obliged to rejoice   30
with those relieved from sickness who rejoice in their new-
found health. But since no one is closer to a man than the
only son of his mother, then if we are bidden for charity's   33

sake to praise the blessings of health conferred upon others, how much more are we bound, first and foremost, to render
3 praise with thanksgiving for those blessings which we know to have flowed abundantly for our own needs from the powers of the martyr, through the grace of God. And thus I, Eysteinn,
6 was at one time carrying out my episcopal duties, by God's will, in the church of the blessed martyr when I was summoned by the master-builder to the top of a wall, to settle cer-
9 tain matters concerning the construction. But the walkway, over which stones were carried, broke under the weight of the crowd that followed us and collapsed. I alone, for my
12 sins, was thrown from that height, to teach me to be more careful of my life and duty, while the others clung to the scaffolding and hoists. My side struck against the narrow
15 edge of a mortar-trough, and the narrowness of the surface that broke my fall made the accident all the more dangerous. My people bore me away like one lifeless, and
18 when after a time I recovered my senses, I was brought to my own bed, where I lay anguished and anxious, aggrieved by a twofold grief. For my broken ribs gave pain, but it
21 pained me no less that I would be unable to attend the approaching ceremonies in honour of the martyr; for in three days it would be Saint Óláfr's day, attended by an influx
24 of people from far and wide. Distressed by these troubles of body and soul, I turned in prayer to my patron, the blessed Óláfr, although doubting my own worthiness, nevertheless
27 with full faith; and as experience shows, not forgetful of his own, he came to the aid of the one who called upon him. For when the festal day had dawned, and the people
30 had as usual been summoned to the celebration of the mass by the sound of bells, I discussed with my attendants whether I ought to be carried to the church, since I was too weak
33 to walk. They urged me to it, and I welcomed their advice, for my own inclination drew me on. At first I hardly

expected to take part in the ceremonies of the mass, fearing that my strength would fail me, but when I entered the
church, the pain abated somewhat, and when I had taken   3
a little time to gather my strength and resolution, I dared
to hope for greater things. Therefore I asked to be robed
again, quickly, that I might appear with the clergy in the   6
procession. When we had arrived at the place where the
procession customarily halted for a sermon, I did not venture to preach, but I attempted, nevertheless, to expound a   9
little upon the Lord Pope's indulgence of sins and remis-
sion of penance. But when, in answer to my prayers, my
strength grew even as I spoke, I drew out the exhortation   12
in the usual—albeit unexpected—sermon. And I carried
out the rites of mass and of the whole ceremony, in such a
way that the effort did not leave me fatigued, but rather   15
the fatigue left me thoroughly refreshed, and, although the
pain had not yet fully left me, my bones were nevertheless fully knit and perfect health was gradually to follow.   18

Concerning a man delivered from madness and from manifold ills of the flesh

In the mountainous district called Rendal, there was a cer-   21
tain man, Þórir by name, who took to wife a woman of his
own station. This man had grown prosperous at that time from
a fortunate inheritance left to him by his parents, but then   24
he was stricken with such a dreadful illness that everyone
marvelled that such manifold wrath of divine chastise-
ment should smite one wretched body. For he was simul-   27
taneously stricken both by paralysis of all his limbs and
by infirmity of mind. Indeed, now that he had became mad,
deaf and dumb, it seemed that nothing proper to a man   30
remained to him save breath alone. Among the many
unheard-of things that occurred during this man's illness, I
deem one more marvellous than all the rest: that he survived   33

for eight weeks—and, after an interval, for three weeks
more—without tasting food or drink or any bodily nour-
3 ishment. Like a lifeless body, this man was brought by his
friends and relations on the hazardous journey to the church
of the blessed Óláfr, where they attended him day and night
6 in the church. From the feast of Saint Michael until the day
when he received the grace of healing, those who had brought
him remained at his side with praiseworthy devotion and
9 admirable constancy, save when they yielded to physical
necessity. Although he could not so much as turn his thoughts
to God, because of his wretched condition, nevertheless
12 we believe that the faith and admirable constancy of his
companions helped him greatly. And thus, when Saint Óláfr's
day came, and there was an innumerable gathering of people
15 from different regions, and when for the salvation of all
the life-giving sacrament was begun before the assembled
multitude, just then he fell from where he had been placed
18 to the foot of the shrine, as if someone had pushed him.
Without delay he rose up so completely healed that you
would have seen no sign of any such affliction in him. And
21 so, coming to the altar to give thanks, he revealed to us
that he did not know in the least what had become of him,
or where he had been from the feast of the blessed Mary
24 until that day. Further, on that same day, before he took a
meal, he visited every church in the city of Niðaróss to
give thanks, moved by proper piety to bear witness to his
27 perfect cure.

How a certain youth was delivered from a phantasmal
illusion

30 A certain youth hired himself out for a year to the farmer
of the farm called Uttorgar. One day he was bound for the
forest to cut firewood, so he took up an axe and a horse-
33 collar and hastened to his work. When he was coming from

the outskirts of the farm into the wilderness of woods and
mountains, he saw at a distance two women approaching
from one side, and they far surpassed the women of that dis-   3
trict in the beauty of their garments and their features. When
he had marvelled at their comeliness and their raiment, he
was so enthralled that he followed them he knew not where.   6
And when he had been led in this way for a long time,
through impenetrable places, they came to a cliff where a
cave lay open in the wall of rock before them. Having entered   9
it, he saw a countless throng of merrymakers and feasters,
as it seemed, with one man sitting in their midst, as if more
honoured than the others, and his authority seemed to rule   12
the rest. When this same nobleman saw him enter, he welcomed his arrival most graciously, and the rest of the merry
crowd rejoiced to receive him well. And although all seemed   15
to welcome him gladly, yet the aforesaid guides of his journey
did so yet more courteously and as if with a warmer ardour, plying him with all sorts of food and drink and finally   18
with other most desirable things of every kind. But although
he was lured by such phantasmal illusions to the destruction of his understanding, nevertheless in his heart he re-   21
membered his faith and never ceased to call upon God and
Saint Óláfr. And when, supported by divine mercy, he had
refused everything that was offered, and relying on God's   24
help had overcome the deceitful wiles of the Enemy, then
the Ancient Adversary, confounded, resorted to open hos-
tilities, seeing that the efforts of his false art were in vain.   27
For the cave, which at first had been a resplendent court, filled
with every luxury, now became frightful; those who had
previously worn human form and fair raiment now became   30
loathsome evil spirits. A fire was also seen raging with sulphurous flame in the middle of the stone floor along the
whole length of the cave. The savage throng surrounded   33
him with clamour and coming from the left side, as if wary

of the right, they drove the trembling youth hither and thither toward the fire. His strength gave way to weariness and
3 hunger, but the weaker he grew in the flesh, the stronger he grew in spirit. For even as he found himself bereft of all human succour, so did he turn with surer hope to the divine
6 mercy. But, behold, as he lamented and prayed aloud for deliverance, the entrance to the cave was illumined by a sudden light; the demons fled; the phantasmal fire vanished.
9 Then a man came, serene of countenance and of speech, saying, 'You have called me, behold I am here.' The youth, however, fearing the earlier deception, answered not a word.
12 He who appeared to him, however, earnestly showing by his holy words that he was on the side of righteousness, said further, 'I am Saint Óláfr whom you have invoked, and
15 you need no longer be troubled by fear, for I have been sent to guide you safely to your home.' But afterwards the youth could neither remember nor relate how he fared, how
18 much time passed, or what took place, from that hour until he entered the building in which he and the other labourers were wont to sleep. But it is certain that he had set out in the
21 morning and returned on the evening of the following day. Whereupon he went to a priest and, when he had unfolded the adventure to him from beginning to end, he devoutly
24 bound himself by oath to life-long service in the church of the martyr, in thanks for the help he had received. And so they both came to us, for at that time we were occupied
27 with church matters in a neighbouring district, in the course of our customary circuit of the diocese. What he had first discussed and decided with the priest, he afterwards con-
30 firmed to me and, as the test of time has shown, what he devoutly resolved to do, he has carried out no less devoutly.

Likewise, a woman who had lost her sight from an af-
33 fliction of the eyes, rejoiced at having obtained a cure a few days before the feast of Saint Óláfr.

At the same time, a certain man of Lundr recovered his sight in the parish church of Hringisakr, a church which has the honour to bear the name of the martyr. Although at first he could not see perfectly, nevertheless, scorning to be led by a guide, he hastened to Niðaróss to give thanks. While he passed some days there preparing for Saint Óláfr's day by devoting himself to acts of thanksgiving and supplications for complete healing, he received a cure, as welcome as it was delayed. But because no one in those parts was acquainted with the aforesaid youth, no one put faith in his words alone. But as Saint Óláfr's day drew near, a multitude gathered from diverse regions, and among them were respected men from his district who acknowledged acquaintance with the aforesaid youth, and confirmed his account with trustworthy testimony.

Concerning a pagan cured of bodily infirmity and spiritual error upon invoking the martyr

Two youths from Estonia, who were newly converted from unbelief to the faith, visited the church of the blessed martyr Óláfr, to pray there. They reported that the radiance of the many miracles performed through the intervention of the blessed martyr Óláfr was growing brighter throughout that still pagan nation, so that the people might more ardently desire the light of faith. One of their memorable accounts was the story related by one of them concerning his pagan father, and this report we deem worthy to be repeated, if it will not be wearisome to your charity. At one time a Christian army invaded those parts and laid waste the accursed temples, along with the people found there. The Christians then judged it a fitting time to preach the word of faith to those who lived there, while the terror of this new Christian victory was upon the land of the unbelievers. Among those who withstood this holy mission, the father

of the aforesaid youth was the most bitter in his opposi-
tion, even while their leader himself exhorted them, now
3 with threats, now with soft words of persuasion. For this
man had recently lost a son in conflict with the Christians,
and this grief was the chief cause of his hatred and resist-
6 ance to salvation. Now, when he would yield neither to
threats nor to blandishments nor to the salutary persua-
sions of his son, who, as we have said, had received the
9 grace of baptism, then finally the divine mercy looked upon
him with compassion and he was seized by a most grave illness. Why make many words of it? As the disease worsened
12 he was worn and tormented until, with his whole body
shrunken together, he seemed to have cast off human form.
And so the soothsayers and those first in conducting the
15 impious heathen rites were called together, that they might
relieve the man's sufferings by their abominable art. But
where divine grace is at work, the evil art is in vain. His
18 son, exceedingly concerned for his salvation, exhorted his
anguished father and mingled salutary discourses with his
ceaseless prayers. Distinguishing between belief and un-
21 belief, he set forth the glory destined for the faithful and
the hell awaiting the heathen. And because the memory of
the blessed martyr Óláfr was renowned in the neighbour-
24 ing districts because of the multitude of his miracles, the
son therefore confidently urged his father to ask for Óláfr's
grace. Hearing, then, the suggestion of this sort of truth,
27 the man hardened his heart, foolishly doubting those things
that are beyond doubt. And so, because he was held fast
by the false religion of his forebears, it was only by means
30 of bodily suffering and the threat of eternal torment that
he yielded, however fleetingly, to the teaching of salvation. Finally, the stronger conquered, for Christ stole away
33 the spoils long kept by the despot. His stubborn paganism
was subdued at last, and in his inmost heart he began to

beseech God's grace and the intervention of the holy martyr. He made a vow and affirmed that if he should find favour
with heaven, he would both accept baptism and visit the   3
church of the martyr as soon as he possibly could. And
when he bound himself by oath to God and the martyr, he
was found worthy to be set free from the chains of infirmity.   6
For it was with upright legs and renewed strength that, mindful of his vow, he eagerly hastened to the grace of baptism.
Having received it, he sought the church of the martyr to   9
perform the acts of thanksgiving, with votive offerings, for
the cure which had been granted him. And there, when he
had marvelled that the practice of Christianity shone with   12
such glory, he was the more confirmed in his faith, having
seen for himself the difference between his adopted religion
and the one that he had left. Thus, tasting how sweet is   15
the Lord, and how blessed the man who places his hope in
him, he added to his former vow that, upon returning home,
he would protect, to the best of his ability, any Christian   18
fleeing from slavery among the pagans there.

Concerning a youth cleansed of leprosy

In the presence of the multitude gathered from various re-   21
gions on Saint Óláfr's day, the son of one of our higher
clergy offered thanks for his healing. For the accomplish-
ment of this wondrous cure let all proclaim with one voice   24
the praise and glory of the One who performs all such glorious
works for the greater glory of his saints. For indeed that
youth had been so beset with the filth of leprosy that the   27
wasting disease was the despair of his relations and the
defeat of his physicians. And truly, as it often happens that
the spirit grows stronger as the flesh weakens, therefore   30
the dearth of human succour made them turn the more confidently to divine compassion. And so the youth and his relations besought the intervention of the martyr to accomplish   33

his cure, vowing, in addition, that they would visit his church
with an offering if divine mercy should be shown them in
3 response to their vow. And then, when their prayers had
been answered, they did their part to fulfil their vow. For
truly the youth was now an utter stranger to infirmity, and
6 his piety overcame his shame so that he chose rather to become a public spectacle than to allow God's glorious miracle
to be hidden in silence because he shrank from display.
9   But neither, I think, ought that matter to be passed over
in silence which was made known to me, here in my church,
by the credible testimony of a certain youth. He had re-
12 cently come from pagan parts, where a great many Christians had gathered to fish, now that Lent was over. When
they made their first casts, and had waited a long while, in
15 vain, for the gift of God, they earnestly discussed what was
to be done. For lying in a narrow inlet in the middle of the
pagan wastes, three or four weeks distant from Christian
18 lands, and disappointed of their expected catch, they were
troubled no less by tedium than by lack of food. But one
day a storm dashed the sea against the surrounding cliffs
21 so that it resounded in the strange winding hollows, and
all the welkin roared, shaken by the dark tempest. Then,
because the fishermen could discern little sign of a calm in
24 the uproar of the elements, they humbly besought with plea
and with prayer the mercy of God and the intervention of
the martyr, affirming as one that they would hold themselves
27 bound to send to the church of the blessed Óláfr the best
fish taken by each ship, if the divine mercy should favour
them. The pagan Lapps who had also gathered there to fish,
30 hearing the vow of the faithful, asked to be admitted as
fellows to this plan, but in such a way that their godlings
should be no less honoured with the fruits of their vow
33 than the blessed Óláfr with the offerings of the faithful.
But since there is no concord between Christ and Belial,

the wretches in their error were spurned. Upon the dawn-
ing of the next day, the darkness of the tempest receded,
along with the darkness of night. When the weather had 3
cleared, calm seas followed, and the calm was followed
by such an abundance of fish that the only question was
how to catch them. But there is something even more won- 6
drous to relate of this miracle. Every day the pagans assembled to fish along with the Christians, but despite all
their skill they were disappointed of their usual catch, as 9
if they were scorned by God. For the catch made by their
boats but barely sufficed for their pressing need of provisions. As a result of the vow made by the Christians, 12
however, twenty-four great fish, in accordance with the
number of ships, came to us on the eve of Easter, together
with the aforesaid account. But since truth is absolutely 15
necessary where the work of God is concerned, we with-
held judgement in this matter until we visited in summer
the borders of the pagan lands, where we received confirma- 18
tion of the youth's account from others who also had personal knowledge of the matter.

A three-year-old bull was brought to the church of the 21
blessed Óláfr. Now when we asked from whence or indeed
why it had been brought, the man whose servant was leading the bull said that it came from the district called Ljoxa. 24
And he gave the reason, saying, 'When in my youth I had
acquired a farmstead and had stocked it with cattle and
other necessities, in accordance with my means, I eagerly 27
hoped, as husbandmen do, that my livestock would multi-
ply. But either barrenness denied them offspring or, when
they did bear, death maliciously snatched away their young. 30
And so I was considering selling my property and trying
my fortune in the town, but my friends and neighbours opposed the idea, saying, "It will hardly go well with those 33
who take to trade late in life without experience." They

advised me rather to turn to God and Saint Óláfr with prayer and vow. Willingly indeed I undertook a vow, promising to Saint Óláfr the first calf to be born every year. What a marvel! For seven years in a row, before this vow, not a single bull-calf had survived, but now, three years after the vow, there are twelve. Two of the ones that belong to Saint Óláfr remain at home to be reared, but this one, since it was older, we have brought as a devout offering of the avowed first-fruits.'

Furthermore, a certain woman, who had lost the use of her legs seven years before from a contraction of the sinews, had been in our township for four years, receiving charity and visiting the church, all the while dragging herself about, doubled over, by the effort of her hands. When this woman kept vigil in the church of the blessed martyr through the night of the Holy Annunciation, she was found worthy to receive perfect health as a message of holy grace.

Not without cause, brothers, are the holy martyrs illustrious far and wide for their miracles in the very places where once they were held in contempt, where, in defence of the faith, they were slaughtered by the ungodly. It therefore happened that on Saint Óláfr's day a certain deaf-mute from a nearby community of Cistercian monks came, along with many others, to the church that was built on the site of Saint Óláfr's martyrdom. While the priest was delivering a sermon of exhortation to the people, this man, overcome by the fatigue of the journey—or rather by divine will— fell asleep, and in a vision he saw a prodigious light glowing in the midst of the crowd with an extraordinary brilliance, and this was followed by a man whose face and raiment shone forth with the splendour of effulgent radiance. When this man drew near, he seemed to speak to him first with a greeting, saying to him, 'If you are seeking a cure, behold, God has healed you.' He asked, 'Who are you, my lord?'

He replied, 'I am the one whom you have invoked.' At that
he awoke, and there before all the people, in proof that he
was completely cured, he proclaimed with clear voice and   3
words the mercy shown him by the power of God and the
intervention of Saint Óláfr. We first learned these things
from the priest of that place, then from the very abbot and   6
monks in whose service the aforesaid youth had previously
been and afterwards remained.

Likewise, on the following Saint Óláfr's day, a small   9
boy recovered his long-lost power of speech in the church
of the martyr, beside his body. Afterwards, during the long
stay made by this same mute in the township the pure clar-   12
ity of his voice proved beyond doubt that he had been cured
of his affliction.

Concerning a boy healed of crippled limbs   15

A certain boy, Karl by name, whose feet were bent back by a
disease of the limbs, was brought by his mother and brothers
to the church of the blessed martyr Óláfr. When he was rest-   18
ing in the hospital devoted to the infirm near the church, he
saw in a dream, around midnight, three men, most radiantly
shining, who were walking through the hall and looking at   21
the bodies of the afflicted. And when they had made a circuit of the whole hall three times, they came once again in
the course of their walking to the bed where the crippled   24
boy was lying. Truly, although it was night-time, such a bril-
liant light filled the whole hall that it was as if the rays of
the sun could be seen through all its walls. Now one of the   27
men stood at the boy's head, another at his feet, and the
third—a short man with a handsome face, whose countenance surpassed the others' in radiance—stood between   30
them in the middle. This man, most beloved brothers, we believe and hold without doubt to have been the blessed Óláfr,
for he was accustomed to appear to men in that guise, as we   33

know from the accounts of many. Now when he was standing there in the middle over the boy he made the sign of the
3 cross above his knees, and, leaning over, he breathed upon
them, then placed his hand upon the boy's brow and wak-
ened him, saying, 'Behold you are now healed, sleep not,
6 rise up quickly.' And forthwith the boy woke, opened his
eyes, and saw that the great light that had been in the hall
was fading away little by little after the departure of the
9 holy men. Then, frightened and all atremble, he began to
cry out, and he desired to explain to those who were with
him what had happened to him. But, mindful of the words
12 of the holy man, he reached his hands to the place where,
before, his crippled feet were wont to press. When he did
not find them pressing there, he began to raise himself with
15 great trust in the mercy of God and in the powers of Saint
Óláfr, to whose abode he had come, and he stood up on
his feet, healed. Giving boundless thanks to God, he walked
18 about freely, and to all those who were staying in the hos-
pice he described what had been done. In the morning, after
the ceremony of mass was completed by God's grace, the
21 boy, who for three years had been trammelled by a disease
so severe that his shins and feet were joined inseparably
to his buttocks, now walked freely wherever he wished,
24 having been released and completely healed by a divine
miracle.

NOTES TO HISTORIA NORWEGIAE

1/2 . . . tus] A large initial and between two and four other letters are missing at the beginning of the text, with the result that the author of the work referred to here as the *Philostratus* has not certainly been identified. While Storm read the surviving letters as *tus* others have read the first letter as an *i* without its dot (e. g. Lehmann 1936–37, 2: 76; Koht 1950, 9; Ekrem 1998a, 22). No work entitled *Philostratus* is known to have existed. Ekrem (1998a, 25–26) suggests that the work referred to here may be a version of the *Imago mundi* by Honorius Augustodunensis (*c.*1110) supplemented by additional material from the Greek *Eikones* by Flavius Philostratus (*c.*200), with the name of the latter work's author having become substituted for that of the work. The letters surviving in the manuscript might then be the last three of Honorius's name (reading *i* instead of Storm's *t*). Or they may be the final letters of the name Solinus (which would fit the manuscript lacuna better); it seems that the author of *HN* may have thought that Solinus was the author of Honorius's *Imago mundi,* either because he found that work together with Solinus's *Collectanea rerum memorabilium* (to which *HN* later refers, see 11/8) in his manuscript, or because reference to Solinus in the *scholia* to Honorius's work led the author of *HN* to believe that Honorius based his work on that of Solinus (Ekrem 1998a, 24). An alternative explanation offered by Ekrem (1998a, 26) would see the *philistratu* of the manuscript as a misreading by the Scottish copyist of *phie tratu,* an abbreviation for *philosophie tractatu*; either Honorius's *Imago mundi* or Solinus's *Collectanea rerum memorabilium* could be described as a 'philosophical treatise'. For the use in *HN* of Honorius's work see Skard 1930, 78–83; Steinnes 1946–48, 17–28.

1/4–1/10 Not by any means . . . many generosities] It was common practice in the Middle Ages to employ the modesty topos in prefaces and prologues and to ascribe a text's existence to the insistence of a patron; cf. also 1/29–1/30 below. On the modesty topos see Curtius 1953, 83–85.

1/12–1/16 to describe . . . both religions] The writer here sets out his three aims. The third of these is unrealised in the work as it survives.

1/18 hitherto unattempted in Latin discourse] This probably implies
that the writer did not know of any Latin history of Norway. In particular it suggests he did not know of the work of Theodoricus, though
he may have known Ari Þorgilsson's lost vernacular *konunga ævi*. It is
also possible, however, to read this as implying that the writer knew of
no work which attempted to fulfil all three of his aims: a geographical
description, an account of Norway's rulers, and an account of the religious struggle between Christianity and paganism. This would leave
open the possibility of the writer's knowing of Theodoricus's work
since it does not contain a geographical description of the region.

1/27 Agnellus] The identity of the dedicatee of *HN* remains uncertain.
The manuscript reads *angnelle* or *anguelle*, which Storm (1880, 72)
emends to *Agnelle*. Most scholars have followed Storm (1880, xxiii)
in identifying him with the Thomas Agnellus who was Archdeacon of
Wells at the end of the twelfth century (see also Koht 1919–20, 110–
11). Paasche (1957, 432) preferred a Franciscan called Agnellus who
was in Oxford in 1224 and he has been another popular candidate (cf.
Ekrem 1998a, 88; 1998b, 50). Bugge (1873, 34–35) suggests Agnellus
could stand for the Norse name Lambi, and identifies him with a prior
of that name at the Norwegian monastery in Elgseter *c.*1240, an identification dismissed by Storm (1880, xxi). Ekrem offers two possible
alternatives: (i) Ormr, abbot of Munkeliv monastery in 1146 (by reading *anguelle* as the vocative of a diminutive of *anguis*, 'snake, worm',
the meaning of ON *ormr* (1998a, 72–73); a candidate also suggested
by Hanssen 1949, 13–15, and Steinnes 1949–51, 184; 1965, 28); (ii)
Eysteinn Erlendsson, Archbishop of Níðaróss 1161–88 (by reading
agnelle, and taking this as an abbreviation for *Augustinelle*, the vocative of a diminutive form of *Augustinus*, the Latin equivalent of Eysteinn
(1998a, 74–75)). This identification is also suggested by Sandaaker
(1985, 86 n. 11). According to Ekrem the identification with Eysteinn
need not rule out his possible authorship of *HN* since non-existent
dedicatees were not unusual in the Middle Ages (1998a, 78).

1/31 teacher's authority] Steinnes (1965, 28) notes that the word for
teacher here (*didascalicus*) has the specific sense of a canon in charge
of the school at a cathedral.

2/9 the first book of the History of Norway] This indicates clearly that the surviving text is only the beginning of the work, though it is uncertain whether what survives is all that was ever written or whether one or more subesquent books have now been lost.

2/11 Nórr] The S text (MS Stock. Perg. 4to nr 18) of the Norse translation of Oddr Snorrason's Life of Óláfr Tryggvason states that *Sa konungr ræð fyrstr Norege er Nór het* (Oddr 83; 'The first king to rule Norway was called Nórr'). Nórr also appears in the section of the late fourteenth-century *Flateyjarbók* entitled *Hversu Nóregr byggðisk* (*Flat.* I 21–24) and in *Orkneyinga saga* chs 1–2.

a very vast country] *Gesta Hamm.* IV.xxxi (30) says of Norway that 'in its length that land extends into the farthest northern zone' (trans. Tschan 1959, 211).

2/14 from . . . , a great river] A manuscript lacuna. Storm (1880, 73) suggests *Albia* or *Albiae* in the light of Schol. 131 (126) to *Gesta Hamm.* IV.xxi (21), or alternatively *Gautorum* or *Gautelf.* Salvesen (1969, 19; cf. 39 n. 3) has [Göta-]elven, following Koht (1950, 11).

2/20 Lapps] Latin *Finni.* Like Old Norse *finnr*, Latin *finnus* may refer either to a Lapp (Saami) or to an inhabitant of Finland (Suomalainen) cf. *MSE* 379 s.v. 'Lapland'.

2/23 Jamtaland] This province is here clearly regarded as outside Norway. *Msk* 353 and Snorri Sturluson in *Msona(Hkr)* ch. 15 hold that Eysteinn Magnússon annexed Jamtaland in 1110, but this is too early a date for the composition of *HN*; *Hákonar saga Hákonarsonar* ch. 11 states that King Sverrir annexed Jamtaland and *Sverris saga* ch. 26 suggests that this was done in 1177. This would fit with a dating of *HN* to before 1177. Ekrem (1998a, 29), however, suggests that *HN* is concerned with ecclesiastical boundaries; Jamtaland did not belong to the Niðaróss archdiocese until 1570.

2/26–27 Kirjalians, Kvænir, Horn-Lapps] Comparison with *Egils saga* ch. 14 suggests that by Horn-Lapps the author here means the inhabitants of Finland between the Kirjalians and the Kvænir. Horn-Lapps also appear in the Icelandic *Hauksbók* (probably written *c.*1306–10; at any rate before Haukr Erlendsson's death in 1334), but by that time they have become man-eating creatures with horns on their heads inspired by Isidore of Seville's description of satyrs (cf. Storm 1880, 74–75).

2/27 people of the two Bjarmalands] Perhaps meaning Bjarmaland on each side of the White Sea (Koht 1950, 11). Saxo Grammaticus (*Gesta Danorum* VIII.xiv.6) refers to *Biarmia ulterior,* thus perhaps implying the existence of *Biarmia citerior* (cf. Storm 1880, 75; Salvesen 1969, 39).

2/31–32 land between the Greenlanders and the Bjarmians] Implies a land connection between these north of the Atlantic Ocean; cf. the twelfth- or thirteenth-century Geographical Treatise preserved in an Icelandic manuscript of 1387: *Af Biarmalandi ganga lond óbygd of nordr-ett, unz vidtekr Grenland* (Kålund 1908, 12; 'From Bjarmaland uninhabited land continues through the north until it joins Greenland').

2/33–3/2 a country of maidens . . . drink of water] Cf. *Gesta Hamm.* IV.xix (19): 'Likewise, round about the shore of the Baltic Sea, it is said, live the Amazons in what is now called the land of women. Some declare that these women conceive by sipping water' (trans. Tschan 1959, 200).

3/2 Greenland] Note that Greenland appears within the description of Norway rather than separately among the tributary islands; this implies a date for the composition of *HN* before 1261, when Greenland began to pay tribute to the Norwegian crown. Greenland is described by Adam of Bremen in *Gesta Hamm.* IV.xxxvii (36) after a description of Iceland.

3/3–3/4 settled and confirmed in the universal faith by Icelanders] Icelandic accounts of the discovery, settlement and conversion of Greenland include *Íslendingabók* ch. 6, *Eiríks saga rauða* and *Grænlendinga saga.* See further Jones 1986, especially 73–114, and Ólafur Halldórsson 1978.

3/7 Skrælings] ON *Skrælingar* ('wretches'). Although *HN* implies that these Skrælings live in Greenland, in *Grænlendinga saga* and *Eiríks saga rauða* this name is given to the inhabitants of Vinland, part of North America discovered and visited by Icelanders and Greenlanders around the year 1000. Ari writes of a people *es Vínland hefir byggt ok Grænlendingar kalla Skrælinga* (*Íslendingabók* 13–14; 'who inhabited Vinland and whom the Greenlanders call Skrælings').

3/16 Decapolis] Greek for 'ten cities'. This name is used of a part of the Holy Land in the Gospels of Matthew (4: 25) and Mark (5: 20). Storm lists the ten Norwegian cities as Niðaróss, Bergen, Oslo, Borg (Sarpsborg), Tunsberg, Konghelle, Stavanger, Véey (Veøy), Skíðan (Skien) and Kaupangr in Sogn (1880, 76; cf. Koht 1950, 13).

3/17 provinces] The Latin term is *patria*, referring here to the area covered by a specific legal code (*lǫg*). On the use of the term *patria* in *HN* see Robberstad 1949–51.

3/18 districts] The Latin term is *provincia*. For lists of the names of districts within the provinces mentioned here and references to the sources see Storm 1880, 77–78, and Koht 1950, 13–14.

4/1 Charybdis and Scylla] A whirlpool and a sea monster in classical legend, also briefly mentioned by Honorius (*Imago mundi* I.xxxv).

4/1–2 whirlpools from which there is no escape] Cf. *Gesta Hamm.* IV.xxxix–xl (38–39).

4/12 *pistrix . . . hafstrambr*] The *pistrix* appears in one reading in Pliny's *Naturalis historia* IX.iv (3) (textual note). The *hafstrambr* is mentioned in a list of kinds of whale in the *þulur* attached to *Skáldskaparmál* in the Codex Regius manuscript of Snorri Sturluson's *Edda* (1998, 127), and in *Konungs skuggsiá* 27, 163.

4/15 *hafgufa . . . hafrkitti*] The *hafgufa* is also mentioned in the *þulur* appended to *Skáldskaparmál* (Snorri Sturluson, *Edda* 1998, 127), in *Konungs skuggsiá* 17 and in *Qrvar-Odds saga* 132. The *hafrkitti* is mentioned in the discussion of different kinds of whale in *Konungs skuggsiá* 16.

4/30–5/6 In the mountainous region . . . cliffs of rock] Koht (1919–20, 112) took this passage as evidence that the author of *HN* was not from the east of Norway, arguing that no one who knew the area around the river in question (the Vorma) or around Oslo could have believed what is stated here. From Storm (1880, 82) onwards scholars have taken the reference to silver here as evidence supporting the belief that the abandoned mining galleries under Gamle Aker church in Oslo represent the earliest mining in Norway. If those mines date back to the second half of the twelfth century they would be by far the oldest in Norway. Recently, however, Moseng has exposed the shaky foundations on which this belief has been based. He points out (1992, 48–49) that *HN* (the only medieval source which might provide evidence of mining at Aker) mentions only silver, not silver mining, and is no more specific geographically than 'close to the township of Oslo', a wide area. According to Moseng (1992, 61–69) there is no definite evidence of mining in Norway before 1490, and no reason to believe the mines at Aker were in operation before *c.*1532. He regards this passage in *HN* as typical of a common kind of medieval 'tall story' about great quantities of precious metals.

5/13 whose skins they wear] Cf. *Gesta Hamm.* IV.xxxii (31): 'They use the pelts of beasts for clothing' (trans. Tschan 1959, 212).

5/19 *ondros*] Not originally, as stated here, a Lappish term, but ON *ǫndrar* (sg. *ǫndurr*). These were skis, specifically those with seal or reindeer skin undersides (cf. Koht 1950, 17).

5/21–23 There is no limit . . . and beavers.] Cf. a similar list of wild animals in *Gesta Hamm.* IV.xxxii (31).

5/28 slave-beaver] The term *biæuerthrel* ('slave-beaver') is used in the Danish *Chronicon Lethrense* (49), written *c.*1170. The description of beavers and their behaviour in *HN* is strikingly similar to descriptions by Gerald of Wales in his *Topographia Hibernica* I.xxv–xxvi, *Itinerarium Kambriae* II.iii, and *Descriptio Kambriae* I.v (the last two of these passages are identical and are more extensive than the first; for translations see Thorpe 1978, 174–77, 227–29). *HN* and Gerald may depend on a lost common source, or simply depend on common oral traditions. See also Bernström 1957.

6/12–7/14 Their intolerable ungodliness . . . in the house] On this description of Lappish shamanistic practices see Bäärnhielm and Zachrisson (1994) and Tolley (1994; 1996). This passage includes the earliest detailed account of a Lappish shamanistic séance. Tolley's comparison of the account with later evidence for Lappish shamanism from the seventeenth and eighteenth centuries demonstrates that despite some misunderstandings on the part of the author of *HN* and some assimilation to Norse rather than Lappish magical beliefs the account is an essentially reliable description of a Lappish séance (Tolley 1994). In a later article (1996), Tolley offers evidence that Snorri Sturluson may have used the description of the Lappish séance in *HN* when describing the supernatural powers of Óðinn in *Yngl.* ch. 7; Tolley does not, however, consider the question of whether Snorri could actually understand a Latin source text (on Snorri's acquaintance with Latin see Faulkes 1993).

6/14 art of magic] The association of the Lapps with magic is commonplace in the Icelandic sagas and elsewhere (e. g. in Shakespeare, *The Comedy of Errors* IV.3.11).

6/16 *gandus*] Like *ondros*, an originally Norse rather than Lappish term (ON *gandr*). Tolley (1994, 143–48) compares Lappish and Norse beliefs about souls and spirits and concludes that the author of *HN* has given the Norse name *gandr* to a spirit with characteristics derived from (i) various Lappish spirits 'both anthropomorphic and theriomorphic, as well as the shaman's free-soul and the dead' and (ii) the Norse *gandr* (including the ability to change into various forms). On the *gandr* see also Tolley 1995.

6/27 under] Storm emended the MS reading *sub* to *super*. The translation here follows Tolley (1994, 136), who dismisses Storm's emendation as 'needless'. The cloth under which the shaman prepares himself is not found in later accounts of Lappish shamanism, although such accounts mention linen hats or veils worn by women assistants; Tolley (1994, 141) suggests the cloth is probably 'a genuine feature which later disappeared amongst men' and which 'may have symbolized the heavens to be traversed'.

6/29–31 with hands extended . . . boat with oars] The lifting up of arms before entering a trance occurs in later descriptions of shamanistic séances (Tolley 1994, 141). The small decorated vessel like a sieve is probably some kind of percussion instrument; Tolley translates 'like a tambourine' (1994, 137); see also his discussion of decorated Lappish drums (1994, 151–53).

6/34–7/2 After dancing . . . as an Ethiopian] Later accounts of Lappish shamanism feature leaping about, and one account from 1672 mentions that the shaman turns black before entering a trance. As Tolley (1994, 141 n. 9) notes, 'given the lack of breathing that is emphasised in many of the accounts, it seems likely that the Lappish shaman did indeed turn distinctly off-colour during trance'.

7/4 he gave up the ghost] Cf. Tolley 1994, 142: 'The author writes of the collapse and death of the shaman without separating them, whereas in fact the shaman must first have collapsed as if lifeless, then sent out his soul, and subsequently have died while in trance as a result of the attack on his helping spirit'.

7/10 whale] Latin *cetus* can refer to any large water creature and Tolley (1994, 137 n. 5) suggests that the usual translation 'whale' may be problematic given the lake setting (unless *stagnum* should be translated 'fjord' rather than 'lake'). The ability of a sorcerer to turn himself into a whale is, however, also found elsewhere in Norse literature; see, for example, *Knýtlinga saga* ch. 3; *ÓlTrygg(Hkr)* ch. 33.

7/11 an enemy *gandus*] Shamanic contests involved fights between animal spirit helpers in which anything suffered by these spirits would be reflected in the shaman who owned them (cf. Tolley 1994, 149–50).

7/22–23 for the benefit of people who live at a greater distance from them] One of several statements implying an intended foreign audience for *HN*.

7/31–32 Scotland] The text has *Hyberniam* (MS *Iberniam*), that is Ireland (so Koht 1950, 20 and Salvesen 1969, 23). The islands in question, however, lie close to the Norwegian coast, thus between Norway and Scotland. A similar misunderstanding of the location of Ireland seems to be evident in *Gesta Hamm.* IV.xxxv (34) and in the report of his voyages which Ohthere made to King Alfred and which was subsequently incorporated in the Old English translation of Orosius's *Historia adversus paganos* (Bateley 1980, 16/1–9). Bateley's note (1980, 193–94) on the passage in the Old English Orosius suggests that Ohthere may have been thinking in terms of sea-routes rather than actual geography and the same may be true of the author of *HN*.

7/32–33 the Orkney islands, more than thirty in number] By the Orkney islands the writer means Orkney, Shetland and the Hebrides (cf. 8/2–4 below and note). For the number 'more than thirty' cf. *Gesta Hamm.* IV.xxxv (34): 'The Orkney Islands, numbering nearly forty, lie close together' (trans. Tschan 1959, 215); and Honorius, *Imago mundi* I.xxxi: *Orcades triginta tres* (thirty-three Orkney islands).

8/1 Orkan] Latin *Orchanus*. He is not mentioned in any other source and may be the author's invention, perhaps by analogy with Nórr (see above 2/11 and note).

8/2 various peoples] Storm (1880, 88) suggests Norse and Celtic peoples (i. e. those living in Orkney and the Hebrides respectively) are meant, but as the statement refers to the past it seems more likely that it is the Picts and Papar mentioned below that the writer has in mind.

8/2–4 two realms . . . rule of earls] The southern isles here are the Hebrides (ON *Suðreyjar*); the northern isles comprising the Orkney earldom included both Orkney and Shetland until 1195 when, following a rebellion against him, King Sverrir deprived the earls of Shetland.

8/5 Each of them pays no small tribute to the kings of Norway] Orkney paid tribute to the Norwegian king from 1150, the Hebrides from 1152 (Storm 1880, 88). The Hebrides were recognised as belonging to Scotland at the agreement of the Peace of Perth in 1266, although they had in practice ceased to be under Norwegian control in 1264. This sentence therefore suggests 1266 as the latest possible date for the composition of the text. Since there is no hint that Shetland does not belong to the Orkney earldom (see previous note) it is likely that *HN* was written before 1195.

8/8 Picts] The earliest known inhabitants of Scotland. With regard to
the statement here that they were 'little bigger than pygmies' Bugge
(1873, 39) draws attention to a long-lived Orcadian tradition to this
effect which is noted by Sir Walter Scott in Note C in his historical
novel *The Pirate* (1996, 346). Scott tells of a clergyman visiting the
island of North Ronaldsay c.1800 who was suspected of being Pictish
because he was 'a very little man, dark complexioned . . . ill-dressed
and unshaved'. Munch (1850, 36–37) suggests that small structures
known in Orkney as 'picthouses' may have suggested that the Picts
must have been unusually short.

8/13–14 the sea dividing . . . Pictland Firth] Now the Pentland Firth. It
is significant that the Firth is said to 'divide' Orkney from Scotland;
this reinforces the connections between Orkney and Norway, and Ekrem
(1998a, 42) takes this as supporting her theory that the opening geographical description in *HN* covers the region which would legitimately
belong to a Norwegian archdiocese.

8/15–17 The greatest of all whirlpools . . . at flood tide] The Pentland
Firth retains a reputation today as a particularly rough stretch of
sea.

8/19–21 the Papar . . . German tongue] An alb is a white linen garment
reaching from the neck to the ankles which is worn by the clergy at
Mass. The Latin term *papæ* is here (wrongly) derived from Low German *pape* (cf. MHG *pfaffe*). Latin *papa*, 'father', was a title used by
priests and is the source of ON *papar* and modern English 'pope'.
Finnur Jónsson (1920–24, II 598–99) and Lehmann (1936–37, 2:75)
believed the author of *HN* could have been a German living in Norway, but it would have been easy for a Norwegian to acquire sufficient
German to make this statement in those parts of Norway, such as
Bergen, which had trading links with Germany (cf. Koht 1919–20,
113). Whereas *HN* says these people were called Papar only because
their dress resembled that of priests, Ari refers to Papar in Iceland
before the settlement by Scandinavians who were Irish Christians: 'Þá
váru hér menn kristnir, þeir es Norðmenn kalla papa . . . þeir váru
menn írskir' (*Íslendingabók* 5; 'Those Christian men were here then
whom Norse people call *papar* . . . They were Irish').

8/21–22 an island still today called Papey after them] Several island-and place-names in Orkney and Shetland derive from *papar*.

8/22–24 It is seen . . . practised Judaism] The source for this remarkable statement is unknown. Storm (1880, 89) suggests that the books referred to may have been fragments of Old Testament books. While this might explain the Judaism, it can hardly account for the idea that they came from Africa. Perhaps this was suggested by the fact that a chapter on Africa follows that on Orkney in Honorius's *Imago mundi* (I.xxxi–xxxii). It may also be significant that one of the features suggesting Pictish race to the early nineteenth-century inhabitants of North Ronaldsay was their visiting clergyman's 'dark complexion' (Scott 1996, 346; cf. note to 8/8 above). Ari's *papar* left books behind them in Iceland, but these indicated that they were Irish and Christian (*Íslendingabók* 5).

8/26 Rǫgnvaldr] Rǫgnvaldr was made earl of Mœrr in Norway by King Haraldr hárfagri and was given Orkney and Shetland as compensation for the death of his son Ívarr on campaign with King Haraldr. Rǫgnvaldr then granted control of Orkney to various other members of his family in turn. See *Orkneyinga saga* ch. 4; *Hhárf(Hkr)* chs 24, 27.

9/2 Gǫngu-Hrólfr] Literally, 'Walk-Hrólfr', a son of Rǫgnvaldr of Mœrr. Identified with Rollo, ancestor of the dukes of Normandy.

9/5 Rouen] Latin *Roda* rather than the usual *Rothomus* or *Rodomus*, probably reflecting the Norse form of the name (cf. Old Icelandic *Rúða*); see Storm 1880, 90.

9/19–29 Having obtained . . . his stepson] This information on Norman dukes and English kings probably derives from the *Descriptio genealogiae ducum Normannorum* in the *Liber de legibus Angliae* (Stubbs 1868–71, II 239–41; see the Introduction above pp. xxii–xxiii). Ellehøj (1965, 161–74), however, argues that the information on Norman dukes in *HN* derives from Ari Þorgilsson's lost *konunga ævi*. In a table at the end of his book Ellehøj provides a useful overview of information on the Norman dukes from several Norse sources in parallel columns.

9/20 count] Cf. 9/26 'count of Normandy'. Latin *comes* rather than *dux*, 'duke'; the words are used interchangeably at this date, but the choice of *comes* here perhaps emphasises Hrólfr's Norse origins by highlighting his relationship to the earls, *jarlar*, of Mœrr (cf. Ekrem 1998a, 43).

9/22–23 The younger Richard was the father of William the Bastard] A generation is missing here and the text may originally have read 'The younger Richard had a son Robert who was the father of William the Bastard' (cf. Storm 1880, 91). William the Bastard is better known today as William the Conqueror (king of England 1066–1087).

9/25–26 Henry, who in the prophecies of Merlin is styled the Lion of Justice] The *Prophetiae Merlini* comprise sections 111–17 of Geoffrey of Monmouth's *Historia regum Britanniae,* and the *leo iustitiae* is mentioned in section 112 (11). Skard (1930, 77) notes that Geoffrey does not explicitly identify the Lion of Justice with King Henry I of England (r. 1100–35); this is, however, made explicit by Orderic Vitalis in Book XII of his *Historia ecclesiastica* (VI 386–89), suggesting that the author of *HN* may have used Orderic's text, though the identification is also made in the *Liber de legibus Angliae* (Stubbs 1868–71, II 241). In *HN* the Latin actually reads *qui in prophetia Merlini regis leo justitiæ prænominatus est,* 'who in the prophecies of King Merlin is styled the Lion of Justice'. Storm (1880, 91) argues that as Merlin is never called a king elsewhere, *regis* here stands for *in historia regum,* a reference to the title of Geoffrey of Monmouth's work. Skard (1930, 77 n. 1), however, draws attention to possible sources for the belief that Merlin was a king; see in particular Geoffrey of Monmouth's *Vita Merlini* 52 (line 21): *Rex erat et vates . . .* ('He was a king and prophet').

9/32–33 subject to the kings of Norway by due payment of tribute] Cf. note to 8/5 above.

10/2–3 'islands of sheep', eighteen in number] Cf. ON *fær,* 'sheep'. The ninth-century Irish writer Dicuil (*Liber de mensura orbis terrae* VII.15) refers to unnamed islands north of Britain filled with innumerable sheep.

10/6 our kings] This implies that the author was Norwegian.

10/8–9 island which the Italians called Ultima Thule] By Italians the writer means Romans; cf. *Gesta Hamm.* IV.xxxvi (35). Adam of Bremen cites several early writers who refer to an island north of Britain called Thule and states that 'This Thule is now called Iceland, from the ice which binds the ocean' (trans. Tschan 1959, 217).

10/10–11 a vast empty land and unknown to men] The author of *HN* is either unaware of traditions recorded by Dicuil (*Liber de mensura orbis terrae* VII.7–13; taking Dicuil's *Thule* to refer to Iceland) and Ari (*Íslendingabók 5*) that Irish hermits inhabited Iceland before the arrival of Scandinavian settlers (Storm 1880, 92), or he deliberately avoids mentioning them so as not to compromise the Norse origins of Iceland and its consequent place within the archdiocese of Niðaróss (Ekrem 1998a, 44–45).

10/11–12 Ingólfr and Hjǫrleifr, Norwegians] In *Íslendingabók* 5 Ari Þorgilsson states that Ingólfr was the first Norwegian to come to Iceland. The much fuller account of the discovery of Iceland in *Landnámabók* 34–47 mentions others who arrived there earlier but did not settle there: Naddodd(r) the Viking (from the Faroes), Garðarr Svávarsson (a Swede) and Flóki Vilgerðarson. Garðarr is said in *HN* to have discovered Iceland (10/15), but his Swedish nationality is not mentioned, perhaps because the author wishes to stress Iceland's Norwegian origins for church political reasons. *Landnámabók* also tells of Ingólfr's sworn brother and fellow-settler, Leifr (later Hjǫrleifr).

10/16 Anbi] Storm (1880, 93) suggests this name may be a corruption of Oddo (= Nadoddr) or Auda (= Auðr djúpauðga, an important early settler of Iceland). Koht gives the form Ambe in his translation (1950, 26).

fifty years] According to Ari wise men said that Iceland was settled in sixty years (*Íslendingabók* 9).

10/18 land of ice] Cf. *Gesta Hamm.* IV.xxxvi (35): 'Thule is now called Iceland, from the ice which binds the ocean' (trans. Tschan 1959, 217).

10/22–23 Mount Hekla which, quaking all over like Mount Etna] The volcanic Mount Etna is mentioned by Honorius Augustodunensis (*Imago mundi* I.xxxv and I.xli–xliii); news of its eruption in 1169 spread throughout Europe (Koht 1950, 27). The Icelandic annals refer to eruptions of Hekla in 1104, 1158, 1206, 1222 and 1300 (see *Islandske Annaler*).

10/32–33 what is reported to have occurred in our own time] Many scholars have agreed with Bugge's suggestion (1873, 35–37) that the eruption referred to here is the one recorded in Icelandic annals for the year 1211, suggesting that *HN* was written soon after that date. But see Storm 1873, 377–78 and Koht 1919–20, 104 for reasons for doubting this.

11/8–9 the book Solinus wrote on the wonders of the world] A reference to C. Julius Solinus's *Collectanea rerum memorabilium* (written *c*.200). At this point, however, *HN* is based not on Solinus but on Honorius Augustodunensis's description of Mount Etna in *Imago mundi* I.xli–xliii. On possible reasons for the reference to Solinus when basing the text on Honorius see note to 1/2 above and the Introduction, p. xxii.

11/10–11 the fountains of the great deep were broken up] Genesis 7: 11.

11/18 Earthquakes] Bede gives a similar description in *De natura rerum* chs 28 and 49 (*PL* 90, cols 249–50A and 275B).

12/4 brings to light . . . in darkness] Cf. 1 Corinthians 4: 5.

12/8 *The origin of the kings*] *HN* is one of a number of sources listing the Yngling kings of Sweden from whom the earliest Norwegian kings were believed to be descended. The surviving texts include: *Ynglingatal*, a probably ninth-century poem by Þjóðólfr of Hvin; a genealogical list at the end of the extant version of Ari Þorgilsson's *Íslendingabók* (27–28) which may be indicative of the contents of his lost *konunga ævi*; Snorri Sturluson's *Yngl.*; genealogies in *Langfeðga tal frá Nóa* in MS AM 415 4to (Kålund 1917–18, 57–58) and *Ættartala Haralldz frá Óðni* in *Flat.* (I 26–27); and, for the kings from Óláfr trételgja onwards, *Af Upplendinga konungum* in *Hauksbók* 456–57. Ellehøj (1965, 114–15) prints lists of the kings from these sources in parallel columns, from which it is clear that *HN* is closest to *Íslendingabók*, though it occasionally shows connections with *Yngl.* and the *Flat.*

genealogy. Various explanations of the relationships between the texts have been put forward. For brief summaries see Magerøy 1976, Rausing 1993; for a full discussion with reference to earlier scholarship and arguing that *HN* used Ari's lost *konunga ævi* as a source, see Ellehøj 1965, 109–41 and 293–94; Krag 1991 offers a reinterpretation of the evidence based on a redating of *Ynglingatal* to the twelfth century. On genealogies with mythological names generally see Faulkes 1978–79.

12/10–11 Þrándheimr, the principal region of Norway] Also the region in which the shrine and cathedral of St Óláfr Haraldsson were situated and the seat of the archdiocese of Niðaróss.

12/11 Ingvi] The Yngling kings are named after him. In the list of kings appended to Ari's *Íslendingabók* (27) Yngvi is a Turkish, i. e. Trojan, king (*Tyrkjakonungr*) in accord with the widespread medieval tendency, following Virgil's *Aeneid*, to trace the origins of western European royal lines back to Troy. In *HN* he is the first Swedish king, either because this was the case in Ari's original version of *Íslendingabók* or because the author of *HN* altered his source at this point. Ari and *HN* agree that Yngvi is the father of Njǫrðr the father of Freyr, but Snorri has Óðinn as the father of Njǫrðr and states that *Freyr hét Yngvi ǫðru nafni* ('Freyr was also called Yngvi'; *Yngl.* 24). *Flat.* I 26 has Óðinn–Freyr–Njǫrðr–Freyr.

12/13–14 Njǫrðr, who fathered Freyr—both these were worshipped as gods by their posterity] Njǫrðr is the first *Svíakonungr* ('king of the Swedes') in the appendix to *Íslendingabók* (27). For this euhemerising explanation of the pagan gods cf. the Prologues to Snorri Sturluson's *Edda* (1982, 3–4), *Hkr* (I 3–5) and *SepÓlhelg* (3).

12/15 Fjǫlnir] The first of the kings to be mentioned in Þjóðolfr of Hvin's *Ynglingatal* (st. 1).

12/23–24 Dómaldi, was hanged by the Swedes . . . fertility of the crops] The form *Domald* in *HN* corresponds to Dómaldr in Ari (*Íslendingabók* 27); *Yngl.* (ch. 15) and *Ynglingatal* (st. 5) have the form Dómaldi. *Yngl.* and *Ynglingatal* also state that he was sacrificed, but only *HN* mentions that he was hanged. The close relationship between the king and the fertility of the land, together with the belief that the sacrifice of a king could secure fertility, were ancient and long-lived beliefs of the Germanic peoples. Lönnroth (1986) discusses Snorri's version of the story of Dómaldi in relation to these beliefs.

12/24 Ceres] A classical rather than Norse deity. The name may be used for the benefit of readers outside Scandinavia as an equivalent of Freyja.

12/31 Alrekr was the father of Hǫgni] *HN* alone has the name Hǫgni (Latin *Hogna*) which appears to be an error for Agni; cf., for example, *Íslendingabók* 27. *HN* agrees with Ari that Alrekr was the father of Agni/Hǫgni, whereas Snorri has them the other way round (*Yngl.* chs 19–20).

12/33–13/1 Agnafit, which is now called Stockholm] The phrase *qui nunc Stokholm dicitur* and the description of the manner of Agni's death are not in the Dalhousie manuscript of *HN* but are added by Storm from the Swedish king lists which depend on an earlier text of *HN*. Evans (1981, 90 n. 3) claims that the reference to Stockholm almost certainly does not derive from the original version of *HN* and points out (1981, 101–02) that the name Stockholm is not found in Swedish sources until 1252. *Ynglingatal* and *Yngl.* give fuller accounts of the events alluded to here; see further Evans 1981.

13/1 Ingjaldr] *Ynglingatal* (st. 12), Ari (*Íslendingabók* 27), Snorri (*Yngl.* ch. 21) and *Flat.* (I 26) all have the name Yngvi. It is not clear why *HN* has a different name.

13/3 Bera (which is *ursa* in Latin)] Both mean 'bear'.

13/4 Jǫrundr] *Ynglingatal* (st. 14) and Snorri (*Yngl.* ch. 24) state that he was hanged by Gýlaugr Háleygjakonungr.

13/10 Aun] The MS has Auchim (emended in Storm 1880, 100 to Auchun), perhaps a mistake for Authun. He is known in other sources as Aun, which Koht suggests might be an abbreviation of Audun or Audvin (1950, 29).

　　Egill, nicknamed Vendilkráki] In giving this cognomen to Egill *HN* agrees with *Íslendingabók* 27, but in *Yngl.* ch. 27 the name, as is more correct, belongs to his son Óttarr who is said in Þjoðólfr's *Ynglingatal* st. 19 to have died in Vendill. Though Egill dies in exile according to *HN* and *Ynglingatal* st. 20, in *Yngl.* (ch. 26) he returns to Sweden and dies there.

13/18 Aðils, or Aðísl] Ari has the form Aðísl (*Íslendingabók* 27), *Ynglingatal* st. 21 and *Yngl.* ch. 29 have Aðils. *Yngl.* ch. 29 has a different account of his death from that given here: Snorri records that Aðils attended a sacrifice at Uppsala and rode around the hall on his horse. The horse stumbled; Aðils was thrown and broke his skull against a rock. Aðils appears in *Hrólfs saga kraka* and, as Eadgils, in the Anglo-Saxon poem *Beowulf*.

13/20 Diana] Another classical rather than Norse deity (cf. 12/24). In *Breta sǫgur* (*Hauksbók* 241) Diana is made equivalent to Gefjun, though Snorri says that the sacrifice Aðils attended was made to the female guardian spirits known as *dísir* (*Yngl.* ch. 29).

13/21 Gautar] *Ynglingatal* st. 23 and *Yngl.* ch. 31 assert that he was killed by Jutlanders (see further Krag 1991, 125–26).

13/24–25 Braut-Ǫnundr who was killed by his brother, Sigvarðr] No other surviving source says that he was killed by his brother (but cf. Krag 1991, 128–29).

13/27 Ingjaldr] Nicknamed (*enn*) *illráði* ('the Wicked') in *Íslendingabók* 27 and *Yngl.* ch. 41.

13/28 *víðfaðmi*] 'Far-reaching'.

13/31 Óláfr, with the nickname 'Tree-feller'] Ari (*Íslendingabók* 27) and *Ynglingatal* (st. 29) count Óláfr trételgja among Swedish kings, as here; in Snorri's *Yngl.* ch. 43 he is a king in Vermaland. Snorri also records a quite different manner of death: in *Yngl.* ch. 43 Óláfr is burned as a sacrifice to Óðinn. The list of Uppland kings in *Hauksbók* (456) begins with Óláfr trételgja.

13/33–34 Hálfdan, with the nickname 'White-leg'] The first of the

Ynglingar to rule in Norway in this text. Ari (*Íslendingabók* 27) and *Hauksbók* (456) agree with *HN* that Hálfdan ruled the Uppland area; *Ynglingatal* (st. 30) and *Yngl*. (ch. 46) claim that he also ruled Vestfold (see further Krag 1991, 133).

14/3 Eysteinn, nicknamed 'Fart'] He appears with the nickname *fretr* ('fart') in a genealogy which though interpolated after the Prologue of *Íslendingabók* largely agrees with the genealogy appended to that work and so may depend on Ari's original version (*Íslendingabók* 3). The cognomen is not found in *Ynglingatal, Yngl.* or *Af Upplendinga konungum* in *Hauksbók*.

14/7–8] Hálfdan who was lavish . . . sparing of food] In the interpolated genealogy after the Prologue of *Íslendingabók* (see preceding note) Hálfdan is called *enn mildi ok enn matarilli*, 'the munificent and stingy with food' (*Íslendingabók* 3).

14/10 Guðrøðr the Hunter-king] Called *veiðikonungr* ('Hunter-king') in the genealogy interpolated after the Prologue of *Íslendingabók* (3). In *Ynglingatal* st. 33 and *Hauksbók* 457 he is nicknamed *gǫfugláti* ('generous'), and *Yngl.* ch. 48 says *hann var kallaðr Guðrøðr inn gǫfugláti, en sumir kǫlluðu hann veiðikonung* ('he was called the Generous, but some called him Hunter-king').

14/12 Hálfdan, nicknamed 'the Black'] His life is recounted by Snorri Sturluson in *Hálfdsv(Hkr)*.

14/14–18 On his way . . . under the ice] Cf. *Ágrip* 2. Other sources, including *Hálfdsv(Hkr)* 91–92, record that the feast was a mid-winter Yule-feast.

14/19 Haraldr hárfagri] Snorri tells in *Hkr* of Haraldr's promise not to cut or comb his hair until he was king of all Norway; when this had been achieved he did have it cut and acquired the nickname *hárfagri*, 'fine-hair' (*Hhárf(Hkr)* 97, 122).

14/25 seventy-three years] Theodoricus (ch. 1) and Ari (*Íslendingabók* 6) state that Haraldr ruled seventy years; according to *Ágrip* (6) he ruled sixty years after winning the whole of Norway. Other sources agree with *HN* that he ruled for seventy-three (e. g. *Nóregskonungatal* st. 9; *Fsk* ch. 5; *SepÓlhelg* ch. 1); cf. further references in McDougall and McDougall 1998, 57–58 n. 18.

14/25–26 sixteen sons] *Ágrip* (4) and *Hkr* state that Haraldr had twenty sons, though their lists are not identical (cf. *Ágrip*, 84–85 n. 10). Thirteen of the sons listed in *HN* are in the list in *Ágrip*; three of those listed here do not appear elsewhere (Jǫrundr (14/34), Yngvarr (15/1), and Hrólfr (15/2)). Comparison of the remaining names with other sources suggests that Gunnrøðr and Guðrøðr (14/30) were originally one and the same person, as also were Sigtryygr (15/1) and Tryggvi (15/2); cf. Koht 1950, 34–35.

14/26 Eiríkr, nicknamed *blóðøx*] The nickname is usually explained as due to the fact that he killed so many of his brothers (cf., for example, *Ágrip* 8), though *Fsk* 79 says that he acquired the name because of his activity as a viking.

14/31–32 Rǫgnvaldr réttilbeini] The nickname means 'straight-leg'.

15/5–6 Gunnhildr, the daughter of the notably foolish Gormr, king of the Danes] Among Scandinavian sources, only *HN* records, as was in fact the case, that Gunnhildr was the daughter of Gormr of Denmark (d. *c*.940; cf. the naming of one of Eiríkr's sons Gormr after him); Norse sources maintain that Gunnhildr was the daughter of one Ǫzurr, that she came from Hálogaland and that she was brought up among the Lapps (*Finnar*; cf., for example, *Ágrip* 8, *Hhárf(Hkr)* 135, *Fsk* 74, *Egils saga* 94, *Njáls saga* 11). *Jómsvíkingasaga* ch. 1 (Blake 1962, 2) records that Gormr was known as 'the Foolish' at first, but later as Gormr the Old or the Mighty.

15/8 six sons] Snorri names seven sons (*Hhárf(Hkr)* ch. 43), *Ágrip* (8) ten. It seems that Gamli and Gormr were originally the same person (Koht 1950, 36; *Ágrip* 88 n.15).

15/14–16 Eiríkr withdrew . . . foster-father] *HN* agrees with *Ágrip* (8, 16) and Theodoricus (ch. 2) that Eiríkr went directly to England (via

Denmark, according to *Ágrip*). *Hkr* (I 152, II 159) and *Egils saga* (176) record that he arrived in England after visiting Orkney. Hákon's foster-father, Æthelstan, reigned 925–39 and Eiríkr is unlikely to have arrived in England during his reign. The *Anglo-Saxon Chronicle* (MS D) records *s. a.* 948 that King Eadred invaded Northumbria in that year to win it back from Eiríkr's control. *Hkr* (I 152–53) says that Æthelstan offered Eiríkr rule (*ríki*, i. e. presumably an earldom) in England (cf. *Ágrip* 16); he is thought to have become ruler there in 847/48.

15/22 Spain] *Ágrip* (16) also records that Eiríkr died in Spain. All other Norse sources agree that he died in battle on Stainmoor in Westmorland in 954.

15/32–34 he nevertheless observed . . . heathen age] In *Ágrip*, *Fsk* and once in *Hkr* Hákon is called 'the Good'.

16/6 Two of their battles] *Fsk* (81–82, 88–93) also mentions two battles, but Theodoricus mentions just one (ch. 4), and *Ágrip* (10–12) and *Hkr* (*Hákonar saga góða* chs 19–31) mention three.

16/26 fourteen years] *Hkr* (I 239) gives fifteen years, Theodoricus twelve (ch. 4), Sæmundr the Wise (as preserved in *Nóregskonungatal* st. 18) nine. *Ágrip* 18 may have either *xv* or *xii* (cf. *Ágrip* 91 n.33). See Ólafia Einarsdóttir 1964, 177–79.

16/31 vǫlubrjótr] This may mean 'breaker of sorceresses' or 'knuckle-cruncher'.

16/34 *klyppr*] 'squarely-built'.

17/2 But . . .] The manuscript shows no sign of a lacuna, but it seems that a section of the text telling how Haraldr Eiríksson died has been lost here.

17/7–8 Hálfdan High-leg was killed by the Orkney islanders] Cf. *Orkneyinga saga* ch. 8 and *Hhárf(Hkr)* ch. 30.

17/8–11 Rǫgnvaldr réttilbeini . . . father's orders] Rǫgnvaldr is said above to have been fostered by a sorceress and to have followed her in the practice of magic (14/32–34). The practice of magic (*seiðr*) was often associated with *ergi,* 'unmanliness' including (passive) homosexual activity, and this may explain the 'degrading practices' referred to here which impel Rǫgnvaldr's father to order his death by drowning (cf. Ström 1974, 8–9, 16–17). In *Hhárf(Hkr)* ch. 34 Rǫgnvaldr is burnt to death in a house by his half-brother, Eiríkr Bloodaxe, but it is probable that *HN* preserves the more original version of events.

17/13 Óláfr and Óláfr] I. e. Óláfr Tryggvason and St Óláfr Haraldsson. The manner in which they are introduced together here may be seen as part of the sustained attempt by *HN* to present Óláfr Tryggvason as just as worthy of canonisation as his sainted namesake (on this see Ekrem 1998a, 60–63; 1998b, 58–59).

17/16 Grenland] Elsewhere, Bjǫrn and his son Guðrøðr are said to have ruled Vestfold (cf. *Hhárf(Hkr)* ch. 35; *Hkr, Haralds saga gráfeldar* ch. 1).

17/20 kúla] 'Knob, ball'.

17/20–21 perpetual king of Norway] At his coronation in 1163/64 Magnús Erlingsson received Norway to rule on behalf of her perpetual king in heaven, St Óláfr.

17/21 Sow] The Latin *scrofa* used here means 'sow', but the Norse form of the nickname, *sýr,* often declines differently from the common noun *sýr,* 'sow', possibly indicating a different original meaning.

17/22–23 Sigvarðr risi (that is 'the Giant')] In Icelandic sources his nickname is *hrísi* (*Ágrip* 4, *Hhárf(Hkr)* ch. 25, *Msk* 56, 190 and *Fsk* 71, 226); with the long vowel this means not 'giant' but 'illegitimate son/bastard' (cf. ON *hrísungr*).

17/28 Óláfr] In *Ágrip* 4 he has the nickname *digrbeinn* ('stout-leg'), but in *Hkr* I 119 is called *Geirstaðaálfr* ('elf of Geirstaðir') after an earlier character of that name who also, according to *Ólhelg(Leg)* 30 had the additional nickname *digrbeinn*.

17/34 a small island] The mound Tryggvareyrr (see 18/2) is modern

Tryggvarör on Tryggvaey (modern Tryggö) to the west of Sótanes (Ranríki). *Ágrip* 26, Oddr 6 and other sources place Tryggvareyrr on Sótanes.

18/8 Saxi, Skorri and Skreyja] All nicknames of men whose names are not now known.

18/11–13 Ástríðr herself . . . Orkney islands] *HN* is the only source to record that Óláfr was born in Orkney; all others have him born in Norway. *Ágrip* 26 has Ástríðr flee to Orkney after Tryggvi's death with a three-year-old Óláfr. In *ÓlTrygg(Hkr)* ch. 1 Óláfr is born on an island in a lake after Tryggvi's death.

18/28–31 when he learnt . . . deprive him of the kingdom] Here the young Óláfr Tryggvason is strikingly compared to the Christ-Child (a 'fatherless boy') and Hákon jarl to Herod; cf. Matthew 2: 1–18. The comparison of Óláfr with the Christ-Child is made more explicitly in Oddr 22–23.

19/10 a kinsman] Ástríðr's brother, Sigurðr Eiríksson was at the court of Vladimir, son of Grand Prince Svyatoslav of Kiev.

19/13–18 When he was about twelve . . . adopted as a son] A slightly fuller account of this deed is in *Ágrip* ch. 18, though that text makes no mention of Óláfr's adoption by the king. Oddr 26–28 provides a much fuller account in which Óláfr is said to have been nine years old.

19/18–19 Practising piracy as a youth] On Óláfr's Viking activity see Jones 1984, 131–33. See also note to 23/24–25 below.

19/23 Jómsborg] Only *HN* and *Ágrip* state that this was Óláfr's winter base. The main source of information on this south Baltic town and the Vikings who inhabited it is the early thirteenth-century *Jómsvíkinga saga*, though it is not clear how much faith may be put in the historical accuracy of its account. See Blake 1962.

19/34–20/1 a small island off Britain] *Ágrip* 28 refers simply to 'a place in England', but most other sources agree that the hermit lived in the

Isles of Scilly. *Britannia* in *HN* corresponds to ON Bretland, referring specifically to the Celtic parts of Britain, here Cornwall. The story of Óláfr's encounter with the hermit and subsequent baptism parallels a similar story told of his namesake Óláfr Haraldsson in *Ólhelg(Leg)* 64. (On the transfer of stories concerning St Óláfr Haraldsson to his namesake in an attempt to promote Óláfr Tryggvason's sanctity see Lönnroth 1963; 1965, 16–18.) Turville-Petre (1967, 135–36) draws attention to a source for the stories in the *Dialogues* of Gregory the Great. The *Anglo-Saxon Chronicle s. a.* 994 states that Óláfr was baptised (or possibly confirmed) at Andover in that year.

20/22 the blessed Óláfr] Cf. 23/17. Ekrem (1998a, 61–62; 1998b, 58–59) adduces this title as evidence of an attempt by the writer of *HN* to advance Óláfr Tryggvason's canonisation. St Óláfr Haraldsson is referred to below as *beatissimus,* 'most blessed' (24/4).

20/22–23 the health-giving change . . . Most High] Cf. Psalm 76: 11 (77: 10).

20/26 Johannes] Cf. *Gesta Hamm.* II.xxxvii (35), Oddr ch. 26 (17). Other sources (*Ágrip* ch. 19, Theodoricus ch. 8) give the bishop's name as Sigeweard/Sigurðr. Oddr (91–92) introduces him as Jón, but later (98, 246) says that he was also called Sigurðr.

Þangbrandr] A prominent early foreign missionary to Iceland. He was rather more successful at making (and in some cases slaying) enemies than converting heathens. See *Íslendingabók* 14; *Kristnisaga* 14–30).

20/28–29 one mind and one mouth] Cf. Romans 15: 6.

20/33 Karkr killed him despicably by night] Parallel accounts tell how Karkr murdered Hákon in a pigsty (cf. Theodoricus ch. 10, *Ágrip* ch. 13, Oddr ch. 21 (15), *ÓlTrygg(Hkr)* chs 48–49). On Karkr's name in different texts and its possible meaning see *Ágrip* 92 n. 40.

21/12–13 the Shetlanders . . . Icelanders] All peoples who came under the jurisdiction of the archdiocese of Niðaróss when it was established in 1152/53. Shetlanders and Orcadians are listed separately here, though in the earlier geographical description the Shetland islands were not mentioned.

21/14 shining in faith . . . ardent in charity] Cf. Romans 12: 10–12.

21/22 the duke of Slavland] Þyri had in fact been married to Búrizleifr (Boleslaw the Brave), ruler of Poland 992–1025. *HN* here agrees closely with *Ágrip* 32, but a slightly different account is given in *Hkr* (I 273, 341–43), Oddr 143–47 and *Fsk* 146–47.

22/3 while sailing past Sjáland] What follows is an account of the Battle of Svǫlðr, the location of which is now uncertain. *HN* follows *Gesta Hamm.* II.xl (38) and agrees with *Ágrip* ch. 20 in locating the battle near Sjáland (Sjælland) in Øresund. See further McDougall and McDougall 1998, 74 n. 113 and references there.

23/1–11 But when the battle . . . an uncertain fact] For similar uncertainty about Óláfr's fate, see Theodoricus ch. 14, *Ágrip* ch. 20, *ÓlTrygg(Hkr)* ch. 112 (citing Hallfreðr vandræðaskáld's *Óláfsdrápa* (*erfidrápa*)). Oddr (chs 73 (61) to 75 (63), 78 (65) to 81) claims that Óláfr escaped the battle, visited the Holy Land and died a monk.

23/16–18 almost uprooted . . . Johannes watered] Cf. 1 Corinthians 3: 6; Matthew 15: 13. See also Oddr 1.

23/23 in Eapolis] The manuscript reads *in ea poli* or *in eo poli*, where *poli* is presumably ablative of the Latinised Greek word *polis*, 'city'. Koht (1950, 49) adopts the latter reading, taking *poli* to refer to Hólmgarðr.

23/24–25 he constantly harassed all the peoples round the Baltic Sea] Óláfr's Viking activities are recorded in Sigvatr Þórðarson's *Víkingarvísur* and Óttarr svarti's *Hǫfuðlausn*.

24/1–2 he was invited . . . to England] Sveinn sailed to England in 1013, but Óláfr did not accompany him. Óláfr had been in England in the army of the Dane Þorkell Strút-Haraldsson inn hávi between 1009 and 1012, then went to France and Spain, wintering in Rouen in 1013–14. On Þorkell's campaign and Óláfr's activities in England see Campbell 1949, 73–82.

24/4 most blessed tyrant] Latin *beatissimus tyrannus*. *Tyrannus* here may have the sense of 'Viking'; cf. Skard 1930, 23, 51; Ekrem 1998a, 43, 61.

Æthelred] Æthelred 'the Unready' (Old English *unræd*, 'ill-advised'), fled England late in 1013 but returned after Sveinn's death on 2 February 1014 with Óláfr among his followers. Æthelred then reigned again until his own death in 1016.

24/19 they eagerly started off together] In fact, Óláfr was not with Knútr; cf. notes above to 24/1–2 and 24/4.

24/22 King Edmund was staying at the time] Æthelred died in 1016 and Edmund was in London that year; Óláfr had already returned to Norway by then. He had, however, been involved in a battle for London in the winter of 1009–10; Sigvatr's *Víkingarvísur* and Óttarr's *Hǫfuð-lausn* celebrate his attack on London Bridge then. See *Ólhelg(Hkr)* chs 12–13.

25/16 Ælfgifu] This is the Anglo-Saxon name used by Emma of Normandy, Æthelred's widow and the daughter of Richard I of Normandy. *HN* is the only foreign source to use this name rather than Emma; see Campbell 1949, 55–58 (especially 56–57). Storm (1880, 123 n. 6), however, suggests the following manuscript lacuna may have provided her alternative name Emma.

25/17 Knútr, nicknamed 'the Hard'] Norse sagas refer to him as Hǫrða-Knútr, i. e. Knútr from Hǫrð in Jutland. The nickname in *HN* agrees with that found in Danish sources. Knútr was the only son of Knútr Sveinsson and Emma/Ælfgifu of Normandy; his half-brother Sveinn was Knútr's son by his concubine, Ælfgifu of Northampton.

25/22 Margaret] She was the sister of Knútr, not of Óláfr of Sweden. Other sources record that Óláfr was betrothed to Ingigerðr, a daughter of Óláfr of Sweden, and that he eventually married her sister, Ástríðr; see, for example, Theodoricus ch. 16, *Ágrip* ch. 25, *Fsk* ch. 30, *Ólhelg(Hkr)* chs 88–93.

25/30 by her had . . .] *Ágrip* (ch. 25) gives Óláfr's daughter's name as Gunnhildr, but other sources (e. g. Theodoricus ch. 16, *Fsk* ch. 30, *Ólhelg(Hkr)* chs 181, 197) give Óláfr's daughter's name as Úlfhildr, which is more likely to be correct.

25/32 Four bishops] Also listed in *Gesta Hamm.* II.lvii (55) as among the many English bishops and priests Óláfr had with him.

25/34 The end] *HN* cannot originally have been intended to end here and in such a perfunctory manner. Ekrem (1998a, 87) suggests that the word *Explicit* may have been transferred here from the end of what was originally Book II, or alternatively that the original reading was *Explicit liber I.*

NOTES TO PASSIO BEATI OLAVI

The Passion . . . Óláfr] The list of contents on the first page of the manuscript (in a probably fourteenth-century hand) calls the work *Passio sancti Olaui regis et martyris* ('The Passion of St Óláfr, King and Martyr'; cf. Metcalfe 1881, 5). Metcalfe's title, retained here, more accurately reflects the contents of the text.

26/1–2 Here begins . . . and martyr] In the manuscript, headings are written in red ink, either in the margin or in the text above the relevant section.

26/1 Passion] The Life of Óláfr with which the work begins is called *Passio* 'Passion' at its beginning, but *Vita* 'Life' at its end (31/28). Storm's edition heads the Life with a description of its contents: 'Sancti conversio; labores ejus apostolici non minus quam regii; martyrium' (1880, 127; 'The conversion of the saint; his work as an apostle no less than as a king; his martyrdom'). The *Hom.* Life is headed 'In die sancti Olaui regis et martiris' (108; 'On the Feast of St Óláfr, King and Martyr').

26/3–28 When . . . torment] As noted by Fabricius (1917, 379–80) and Skard (1970, 83), the opening of the Life has similarities (including the reference to Jeremiah) with the *proemium* to the Life of the Danish protomartyr, St Knútr Sveinsson (r. 1080–86) written in the 1120s by Ailnoth of Canterbury (cf. *VSD* I 82–84); these similarities suggest a literary connection between the two works, but this is denied by Gunnes (1996, 213).

26/3–5 Norway . . . the south] This seems to imply an expected audience for the text outside Norway ignorant of that country's location. The *Hom.* version of the Life begins with a slightly different description of Norway, omitting the reference to Denmark (*Hom.* 108) and does not mention Óláfr until after describing the heathen state of Norway and God's sending of missionaries there (*Hom.* 108 line 30).

26/5–7 the feet . . . good things] Romans 10: 15; cf. Isaiah 52: 7, Nahum 1: 15. This phrase is not in *Hom.* On the role of English missionaries in Norway see Abrams 1995.

26/14 Jeremiah] Cf. Jeremiah 1: 13–14. *Hom.* does not include this reference to Jeremiah (cf. *Hom.* 108). Metcalfe (1881, 67) notes a resemblance here between the *Passio* and a passage on the northern rebellion of William the Conqueror's reign in a collection of the miracles of St John of Beverley, *Miracula sancti Johannis eboracensis episcopi* by William Ketell of Beverley, written *c.*1150 (Raine 1879–94, I 265). Eysteinn (or an earlier reviser of the *Passio*) may have added the allusion to Jeremiah after encountering Ketell's work and after the vernacular translation preserved in *Hom.* had been made (cf. Holtsmark 1956, 21). Skard (1930–33, 367), however, denies the likelihood of any influence from Ketell's work.

26/15 boaster] *Hom.* (108) has *fianden* and *anscoti* (both = 'adversary; devil'); in Isaiah 14:12 it is Lucifer.

26/16–18 I will exalt . . . the north] Isaiah 14: 13. The association of the north with evil, inspired by biblical passages such as this and the one from Jeremiah referred to in the note to 26/14 above, was commonplace in the Middle Ages. For 'stars of God' (Vulgate *astra Dei*), *Hom.* has *himintungl*, 'stars of heaven/the sky' (*Hom.* 108). *Hom.* continues the quotation from Isaiah: 'ok likiasc hinum á-gæzta guði' ('and [I shall] be like the most high God'; cf. Isaiah 14: 14).

26/18–19 who builds . . . the north] Psalm 47: 3 (48: 2).

26/24–25 the truth . . . Christ Jesus] Cf. John 1: 17.

26/30–27/1 Although a pagan . . . righteousness] *Hom.* has no reference to Óláfr's character before he was converted.

27/1–4 Having learnt . . . Rouen] Adam of Bremen implies that Óláfr was converted to Christianity in England (*Gesta Hamm.* II:lvii (55)). The eleventh-century Norman historian William of Jumièges states that Óláfr was baptised in Rouen, the capital of Normandy (*Gesta Normannorum Ducum* v.12; van Houts 1992–95, II 26–29). Icelandic sagas record a different tradition: in *ÓlTrygg(Hkr)* ch. 60 the three-year-old Óláfr is baptised during Óláfr Tryggvason's missionary campaign to Hringaríki with the king as sponsor (though Snorri does record that Óláfr visited Rouen during his youth as a viking, *Ólhelg(Hkr)* ch. 27); *Ólhelg(Leg)* ch. 8 has a similar account, though there Óláfr is said to be five years old. Theodoricus says that some think Óláfr and his mother were baptised during Óláfr Tryggvason's missionary campaign in Upplǫnd, and others believe he was baptised in England, but that he has read in the 'History of the Normans' (i. e. William of Jumièges) that Óláfr was baptised in Rouen by Archbishop Robert (Storm 1880, 22; McDougall and McDougall 1998, 17).

27/4–5 health-giving font] Cf. Titus 3: 5.

27/5 became a different man] 1 Kings (1 Samuel) 10: 6.

27/5–6 the apostle] St Paul.

27/6 buried . . . death] Romans 6: 4. The translation in *Hom.* echoes Romans 6: 6 rather than 6: 4, presumably reflecting an earlier lost version of the *Vita* (cf. Holtsmark 1956, 21).

27/7–8 Forgetting . . . to come] Philippians 3: 13.

27/9 walked in newness of life] Romans 6: 4.

27/12 poor in spirit] Cf. Matthew 5: 3.

27/21 the grace . . . his lips] Psalm 44: 3 (45: 2).

27/30 in the midst . . . perverse nation] Philippians 2: 15.

28/3 the righteous . . . a lion] Proverbs 28: 1. This comparison with a lion and the following reference to Job (see next note) are not in the *Hom.* version (cf. *Hom.* 109).

28/4–6 following the example . . . terrify him] cf. Job 31: 34.

28/8 Gracious Jesus] This rhetorical apostrophe is absent from *Hom.* (cf. *Hom.* 109).

28/10–12 Without doubt . . . his sake] Philippians 1: 29.

28/18–19 trusting in their own folly . . . her whelps] Proverbs 17: 12.

28/24–25 the number . . . day by day] Cf. Acts 2: 47; 5: 14.

28/25–26 Idols . . . overthrown] Cf. 4 Kings (2 Kings) 23: 12–14.

28/28–29 The worshippers . . . were confounded] Cf. Isaiah 42: 17.

28/31 all iniquity stopped her mouth] Psalm 106 (107): 42.

29/2–17 In his reign . . . fellow-men] Having detailed Óláfr's contribution to his country's religious life the text now portrays him as an ideal (secular) ruler, a *rex iustus.*

29/3 nothing of tyranny] Contrast the description of Óláfr in *Historia Norwegiae* as *beatissimus tyrannus,* 'most blessed tyrant' (Storm 1880, 121; 24/4 above; *tyrannus* perhaps has the sense 'viking' there).

29/7 proclaimed laws . . . civil] Óláfr, like Kings David of Israel and Alfred of England, acquired a reputation as a law-giver; cf. Theodoricus ch. 16; *Ólhelg(Leg)* chs 29, 38; *Ólhelg(Hkr)* ch. 58. References to the law of St Óláfr may be found in lawbooks, especially *Gulaþingslǫg*: see Keyser *et al.* 1846–95, V 417; see also Blom 1981, 31–33.

29/9–15 In them he assigned . . . rigour of law] Archbishop Eysteinn was a firm supporter of Gregorian reform in Norway, with its strict demarcation of powers between church and monarch, and this passage may be read in the light of Eysteinn's conflict with King Sverrir. Gunnes (1973, 6) suggests that the sentence 'In them . . . their bishops' is inspired by a passage from Hugh of St Victor, *De sacramentis christianae fidei* II.2.6 (*PL* 176, col. 419), written in 1139. Eysteinn had close links with the Augustinian canons of St Victor in Paris, studying there before becoming chaplain to King Ingi and probably visiting them again in 1160; Gunnes therefore takes this allusion to Hugh's work as evidence for Eysteinn's authorship of the *vita* section of the *Passio Olavi* (1973, 7).

29/25 Russia] Other accounts of Óláfr's exile in Russia include Theodoricus chs 16, 18; *Ágrip* ch. 26; *Ólhelg(Leg)* chs 69–72; *Ólhelg(Hkr)* chs 181, 186–92. Óláfr stayed with Jaroslav, ruler in Kiev (ON Jarizleifr, r. 1019–54), who was married to Óláfr's sister-in-law Ingigerðr (to whom Óláfr had earlier been betrothed), the daughter of King Óláfr of Sweden. Jaroslav was half-brother and promoter of the cults of Russia's protomartyrs, Princes Boris and Gleb (d. 1015). Óláfr's son Magnús remained in Russia until recalled to become King of Norway in 1035, after which he encouraged his father's cult, raising the interesting possibility that he learned of the political usefulness of royal saints' cults while staying with Jaroslav; on Saints Boris and Gleb see Hollingsworth 1992, xxvi–lvii, 3–32; on the politics of royal sanctity in Scandinavia and Russia see Hoffmann 1994 and Poppe 1994 respectively.

29/34 talent] cf. the Parable of the Talents in Matthew 25: 14–30. This allusion is absent from *Hom.* (cf. *Hom.* 110).

30/4–6 He stayed . . . and patience] *Ólhelg(Leg)* ch. 69 states that Óláfr stayed with Jaroslav in Hólmgarðr (Novgorod); if he left this kind of favourable impression there this might explain the dedication of a church to Óláfr in Hólmgarðr. Miracles which took place at that church are recorded below, 47/3–17, 51/23–52/14.

30/9 by way of Sweden] Other accounts (Theodoricus ch. 18; *Ólhelg(Leg)* ch. 72; *Ólhelg(Hkr)* chs 196–98) tell how Óláfr collected troops in Sweden.

30/14 wholesome instruction] 1 Timothy 1: 10; 2 Timothy 4: 3.
  Clad in . . . faith] 1 Thessalonians 5: 8.

30/14–15 girded . . . word of God] Ephesians 6: 17. The version of this passage in *Hom.* follows more closely Ephesians 6: 14, 16, 17.

30/15–17 in honour . . . the left] 2 Corinthians 6: 8.

30/22 the labourer . . . his hire] Luke 10: 7.

30/25–26 the king might see . . . in his beauty] Isaiah 33: 17.

30/26–27 that particular part . . . holy body] I. e. Þrándheimr, the region around Niðaróss.

30/32–33 gathered together . . . his anointed] Psalm 2: 2, cf. Acts 4: 26. Cf. Theodoricus (Storm 1880, 39; McDougall and McDougall 1998, 29). This is the only close verbal parallel between the *Passio* and Theodoricus and may be due to independent use of the Scriptural source.

31/2 a certain Knútr] Knútr inn ríki Sveinsson, King of Denmark and England (r. 1016–35). The *Passio* marginalises the internal Norwegian political background to Óláfr's death, as is evident from a comparison with the additional information given at this point in the vernacular translation in *Hom.* (which, however, does not mention Knútr): 'En forenge fyrir þvi liði. þa var næmdr Cálfr Arnasonr. maðr cynstór. illr ok utrvr sem aller verða drotens svicarar. Sa hinn illi maðr var í svicum við hann. ok com í mote honum með micclum flocce. ok vann hann þa niðings-værc á sinum lánar-drotne er hann var famennastr fyrir staddr' (*Hom.* 111); 'And the leader of that troop was called Kálfr Árnason, a man of noble descent, evil and faithless like all who betray their lord. This evil man was a traitor to him and came against him with a large company and performed a despicable deed against his liege lord when he was before the place with the fewest men.'

31/5 Stiklarstaðir] *Hom.* notes that this is in the Veradalr region (*Hom.* 111). A church was later built at the scene of Óláfr's martyrdom (cf., for example, 52/16–19, 72/24–25 below)

31/19–20 the spears of the wicked] *Hom.* (111) specifically mentions wounds which Óláfr received in his knee and cheek before dying. Theodoricus (ch. 19) notes that there are varying reports about how and by whom Óláfr was wounded; in both *Ágrip* (ch. 31) and *Ólhelg(Leg)* (chs 81–82) Óláfr receives a wound in the knee or leg and is then dealt a death-blow; in *Ólhelg(Hkr)* (ch. 228) Óláfr receives three wounds, in his left leg, abdomen, and the left side of his neck.

31/20 He died . . . the faith] Hoffmann (following Graus 1965, 428) identifies kings killed in battle against heathens as one of four types of Germanic royal saint (1975, 14). Óláfr was assimilated to this model although there would have been Christians and pagans on both sides and his opponent Knútr was closer to the papacy than was Óláfr (cf. Hoffmann 1975, 77–78).

31/21–23 four days . . . Lord's incarnation] The manuscript reading *octobris* must be an error for *augusti*, or possibly for *mensis octavi* (cf. Gjerløw 1967, col. 562). Whereas the *Passio* here gives the year as 1028, Ari (*Íslendingabók* 19) and Snorri (*Ólhelg(Hkr)* ch. 235) imply that the year was 1030. *Ólhelg(Leg)* ch. 88 appears to give a date in July 1030, though not the 29th. Theodoricus ch. 19 gives the year as 1029 (followed by *Ágrip* 44; see 100 n. 98). This may be an attempt at compromise between 1028 and 1030 (cf. *Fsk* xxxvi). The *Passio*, Theodoricus and Snorri, however, all agree that Óláfr died on a Wednesday. 29 July fell on a Wednesday in 1030 (see Ólafía Einarsdóttir 1964, 75–76, 185–86, 329). An eclipse of the sun, to which Sigvatr Þórðarson refers in his *Erfidrápa* (st. 30), occurred on 31 August 1030 (cf. Liestøl 1932, especially pp. 1–17, 27–28). The *Anglo-Saxon Chronicle* (MSS C, E) also gives the year of Óláfr's death as 1030. *Hom.* gives the year of the martyrdom as 1024, which is clearly wrong; it also notes that the day of Óláfr's death is now observed as his feast day: 'ok þat mund árs er nu halda aller cristnir menn hotið hans siðan. er vér cøllum Olafs-messo hina fyrri' (*Hom.* 111; 'and that will now be held in honour by all Christian men as his feast day, which we call the former Óláfr's mass').

31/24–25 the peace . . . all understanding] Philippians 4: 7.

31/26–27 to whom is honour . . . and ever.] Romans 16: 27.

NOTES TO MIRACULA BEATI OLAVI

32/5 those who hear] This implies public reading of the text (cf. 54/29 and note below). This sentence neatly sums up the aims of the hagiographer (see Introduction pp. xli–xlv).

32/9–21 Indeed . . . tasted] Both Storm's edition of *Acta Olavi* (where 'It is fitting . . . his saint' introduces Cap. II but 'Indeed . . . tasted' is Cap. I.xi) and *Hom.* place this miracle story towards the end of the *vita* (where it belongs chronologically) and before announcing the beginning of the *miracula*. Accounts of Óláfr's dream of ascending a ladder to heaven occur in a number of sources, including *Gesta Hamm.* II:lxi (59) Schol. 41 (42); *Geisli* stt. 15–16; *Hom.* 111; *Ólhelg(Leg)* ch. 78; *Ólhelg(Hkr)* ch. 214. The *Passio* (32/19–20) states that Óláfr had dreamed of a ladder previously but does not explicitly say that he sees one on this occasion (unlike *Hom.*).

32/10 the Lord Jesus] *Passio Olavi* here agrees with *Geisli* and *Hom.*, but *Gesta Hamm.* does not mention any figure in the dream (*Gesta Hamm.* II:lxi (59) Schol. 41 (42)).

32/11 with fair . . . of solace] Zechariah 1: 13.

32/22–33/5 Cf. *Geisli* stt. 22–24; *Acta Olavi* II:i; *Hom.* 112 (i); *Ólhelg(Leg)* ch. 87 (twice); 89; *SepÓlhelg* ch. 236; *Ólhelg(Hkr)* ch. 236.

33/6–34/17 Cf. *Geisli* stt. 31–34; *Acta Olavi* II:ii; *Hom.* 112–13 (ii); AM 325, 35 (1r1–5); *Ólhelg(Leg)* chs 90–91; *SepÓlhelg* ch. 266; *HSig(Hkr)* chs 54–55. On Óláfr's early cult in the Irish Sea region see Hudson 1988, 258–89, 265 n. 8. This and the next miracle are linked by the theme of granting assistance in battle.

33/9 Guthormr] Although said only to be Norwegian and a nephew of St Óláfr here, Snorri provides him with a genealogy (*Ólhelg(Hkr)* ch. 128; cf. *HSig(Hkr)* ch. 54): Guthormr's mother, Gunnhildr, is the daughter of Ásta Guðbrandsdóttir, mother of St Óláfr and of Haraldr harðráði Sigurðarson. Guthormr's residence in Dublin may be explained by close ties between Dublin and Scandinavia (Hudson 1988, 261–63).

Snorri places this miracle in the reign of Haraldr harðráði (1045/48–66) and recounts it before an event of 1061 (Haraldr's invasion of Jutland the summer before the Battle of the River Niz, *HSig(Hkr)* ch. 60); Hudson suggests the disruption caused to the narrative by Snorri's placing of this event indicates he may have been accommodating information he had on the date of the miracle (1988, 259, 263).

33/13 Margaðr, the king of Dublin] Latin *margodo*, cf. Margodus, *Hom.* 112; Mardagus, *Ólhelg(Leg)* 210; Margaðr, *Hkr(HSig)* chs 54–55. Identified by Munch (1855, 171–72) with Echmarcach Rǫgnvaldsson (king of Dublin 1036–38, 1046–52), an identification accepted by Metcalfe (1881, 75), Skard (1970, 85), Bjarni Aðalbjarnarson (*Hkr* III 135 n. 1), and Heinrichs *et al.* (*Ólhelg(Leg)* 211 n. 163). Hudson argues that Margaðr is more likely to be an Old Norse form of the Irish name Murchad (1988, 259–60). One Murchad, son of Diarmait mac Máel na mbó, ruled in Dublin during the latter part of Haraldr harðráði's reign and until 1070; he was also, like Margaðr in the *Passio*, a naval commander who led raids in the Irish Sea (see Hudson 1988, 260–61, with references). Hudson's identification of Margaðr with this Murchad fits with Snorri's implied date for the miracle of *c.*1061; Hudson suggests that Guthormr may have accompanied Murchad on his raid on the Isle of Man in 1061 (when he received tribute from Echmarcach Rǫgnvaldsson, who was by then king of Man) before they fought each other over the spoils (1988, 263).

33/31 the vigil of the feast] The saga accounts imply that the commemoration of Óláfr's martyrdom (29 July) rather than of his translation (3 August) is referred to (cf. Hudson 1988, 265 n. 5).

34/8 he attacked] *Geisli*, AM 325 and Snorri record that this battle took place in the Menai Strait.

34/9 overthrew] Latin *prosternit* (*prostravit*, Storm 1880, 134; cf. Hudson 1988, 261). Snorri records that Margaðr *fell*, 'died', in the battle (*HSig(Hkr)* 136). The identification of Margaðr with Murchad mac Diarmata depends on Murchad escaping from this defeat, as he died in Dublin in 1070; Hudson explains Snorri's verb as a mistranslation of the Latin, but it is in fact unlikely that Snorri made direct use of the Latin text; he does seem to have used a text similar to *Hom.* (cf. Whaley 1987, 328–29), which reads 'þa lagðe hann við iorðu konungen' (*Hom.* 113; 'then he laid the king to the earth', i. e. killed him). A similar difficulty arises, however, with the identification of Margaðr with Echmarcach Rǫgnvaldsson, since he died in Rome in 1065 (cf. Hudson 1988, 260).

34/13 a silver cross] Snorri implies that it was still in the cathedral when he was writing (i. e. *c.*1220–30; *HSig(Hkr)* 137).

34/17 Óláfr's holy merits] The *Passio* lacks a doxology at the end of this miracle and an introductory clause at the beginning of the next which are found in *Hom.* 113 and *Ólhelg(Leg)* 212.

34/18–35/27 Cf. *Geisli* stt. 51–56; *Acta Olavi* II:iii; *Hom.* 114 (iii); AM 325, 35 (1r5–9); *Ólhelg(Leg)* ch. 92; *SepÓlhelg* ch. 267; *Hákherð(Hkr)* ch. 21, *Msk* 65–66. Of the miracles found in both the *Passio* and *Geisli* this is the only one to appear in a different position in the two works; it is the thirteenth and penultimate miracle in *Geisli*, preceding the healing of the English priest, in what Holtsmark calls its original place (1956, 23).

34/20–22 Not content . . . the earth] Cf. Psalm 18: 5 (19: 4).

34/24 the emperor] In *Hkr* the emperor is named as *Kirjalax* (*Hákherð(Hkr)* ch. 21), that is *Kyrios Alexios* (Lord Alexios), whom Metcalfe (1881, 76 n. 6) identifies with the Emperor Alexios I Komnenos (r. 1081–1118). In Icelandic sources, however, the name Kirjalax also became attached to other Byzantine emperors, particularly to Alexios's son, John II Komnenos (r. 1118–43; co-regent from 1092; see Blöndal/Benedikz 1978, 122), and Blöndal/Benedikz (1978, 148–50) take the battle referred to here to be the Battle of Beroë in 1122, in which John II defeated the Pechenegs (a Turkish tribe who lived along the lower Danube) on his Balkan frontier. Sandaaker, however, notes that *Msk* 65 associates the miracle with Haraldr harðráði and has a blind king see Óláfr though no one else can see him, while AM 325 states that the enemy were *bolgar* 'Bulgarians', not Pechenegs;

he therefore argues that the battle is more likely to have been that in
which the Bulgarian revolt of 1040–41 led by Peter Deljan was sup-
pressed, although the story changed over time so that the enemy became heathen in later versions and the motif of the blind king seeing
St Óláfr lost its importance (Sandaaker 1991). Norse sources state that
the battle took place at Pétzínavellir. Blöndal/Benedikz suggest that
'this curious place-name probably derived from the name of the war-
ring tribe [i. e. the Pechenegs] rather than from any real field-name
nearby' (1978, 148, cf. 153); Sandaaker, however, identifies it with
the plains of Pčinja, a tributary of the River Vardar in Macedonia.
Geisli, AM 325 and Snorri state that 450 (i. e. 540) Varangians
(Scandinavian mercenaries in the service of the Byzantine emperor;
see note to 51/24 below) were involved, and that the odds against the
Byzantine forces were sixty to one (for the last point cf. *Ólhelg(Leg)*
214). For a comparison of Norse and Greek accounts of the battle see
Blöndal/Benedikz 1978, 148–53. In *Geisli* and *Hkr* the account of this
battle is preceded by a miracle which explains how the Byzantine
emperor came to know of St Óláfr: a sword called Hneitir which Óláfr
discarded when fatally wounded in the Battle of Stiklarstaðir ends up
in the possession of a Varangian, from whom the Emperor learns about
St Óláfr and buys the sword, installing it above the altar of the Byzantine church of St Óláfr attended by the Varangians (*Geisli* stt. 43–45;
Hákherð(Hkr) ch. 20; cf. next note).

35/3–5 a church . . . Virgin Mary] Greek sources attribute John II's
victory at Beroë to the intervention not of St Óláfr, but of the Virgin
Mary (cf. Blöndal/Benedikz 1978, 151, 185). Whereas AM 325 and
Hákherð(Hkr) ch. 21 state that this church was dedicated only to St
Óláfr, the Bergsbók hybrid text of Snorri's saga of St Óláfr states that
the dedication was to both Óláfr and Mary (*SepÓlhelg* 834). The statement at this point in the *Passio* that the church is to be dedicated to
Óláfr and Mary is apparently contradicted below, where it is said the
emperor has a church built in honour of Mary only (35/18–19). Blöndal/
Benedikz believe it 'highly probable' that there was a church constructed by the Varangians in Constantinople consecrated to the Virgin Mary and St Óláfr (1978, 152–53). The oldest church known from
Byzantine sources to have been used by the Varangians was dedicated
to Mary; Blöndal/Benedikz suggest 'it was probably this one that was

built after John II's victory at Beroë' (1978, 186), and that 'it is more than likely that it contained a chapel dedicated to St Olaf, over whose altar the sword [Hneitir; see previous note] was placed' (1978, 153).

35/7–8 The martyr appeared . . . the Christians] Sandaaker suggests that this miracle story may be influenced by Byzantine cults of warrior saints such as Saints George and Demetrios (1991, 92, 96); on such cults see Delehaye 1909. In a miracle which is not recorded in the *Passio Olavi* Óláfr grants victory to his son Magnús góði in battle against pagan Wends at Hlýrskógsheiðr (*Geisli* st. 28; *Ágrip* ch. 38; Theodoricus ch. 24; *Fsk* ch. 50; *Msk* 42–44; *Mgóð(Hkr)* chs 27–28). Two other Scandinavian royal saints also grant supernatural assistance in battle: St Magnús of Orkney, whom late medieval traditions credit with decisive interventions in the Battle of Bannockburn in 1314 (Batho and Husbands 1936–41, II 277) and the Battle of Summerdale in 1529 (Cody and Murison 1888–95, II 218–19); and St Knútr lávarðr, who assists Valdimarr Knútsson of Denmark against the pagan Wends (*Knýtlinga saga* 292).

35/8–9 an illustrious standard-bearer] Norse texts have him riding on a white horse (e. g. *Msk* 65; *Hákherð(Hkr)* ch. 21), an animal also associated with Saints George and Demetrios (Sandaaker 1991, 92).

35/28–36/29 Cf. *Geisli* stt. 35–36; *Acta Olavi* II:iv; *Hom.* 115 (iv); *Ólhelg(Leg)* ch. 93; *SepÓlhelg* ch. 268; *HSig(Hkr)* ch. 56.

35/29 Denmark] This miracle story suggests that the cult of St Óláfr became established in Denmark from an early date (cf. 'Now it happened . . . great reverence', 36/6–9 below).

official] Latin *prepositus*. Probably a reeve, bailiff or local magistrate (Storm 1880, 136; Metcalfe 1881, 78); the vernacular texts refer to him as *greifi*, 'count'.

35/30 the unjust judge] The parable of the unjust judge is in Luke 18: 1–8.

35/30–31 feared not God . . . regarded man] Luke 18: 2.

36/26–27 changed to stones] These stones appear in iconography associated with the saint; Icelandic churches dedicated to Óláfr had stones carved from lava as reminders of this miracle (cf. *DI* I 710 n. 2).

36/30–37/19 Cf. *Geisli* stt. 37–38; *Acta Olavi* II:v; *Hom.* 115–16 (v); AM 325, 35–36 (1r9–25); *Ólhelg(Leg)* chs 94; 101; *SepÓlhelg* ch. 276; *Msona(Hkr)* ch. 30. This and two of the next three miracles are linked by the healing of tongues which have been cut out.

36/32 A certain boy] In the second of the two versions of this miracle in *Ólhelg(Leg)* (ch. 101) the boy's name is given as Kolbeinn and that of the person who cut out his tongue as Þóra, mother of King Sigurðr munnr (who died in 1155). A monk of Niðaróss called Hallr is said to have seen the healed boy (*Ólhelg(Leg)* 229). Snorri also gives the boy's name but says that Þóra was the mother of Sigurðr Jórsalafari (d. 1130; *Msona(Hkr)* ch. 30).

37/4 loud lamentations] The difficulty of doing this after having had his tongue cut out is here disregarded; contrast the behaviour of the English priest below ('His mouth . . . more tellingly' 38/31–32).

37/10 a man of middle height] The first of three allusions to Óláfr's medium height (cf. 43/22, 56/21); at 73/29 he is described as short. Ideally a king would be a tall man (cf. *Msona(Hkr)* ch. 21). In Norse sources Óláfr is nicknamed *inn digri*, 'the stout' or 'fat'. On physical descriptions in Old Norse literature see Helgi Þorláksson 1979, especially pp. 174–80.

37/20–26 Cf. *Geisli* stt. 40–41; *Acta Olavi* II:vi; *Hom.* 116 (vi); AM 325, 36 (1r25–9); *Ólhelg(Leg)* chs 99, 101; *SepÓlhelg* ch. 277; *Hsona(Hkr)* ch. 24.

37/20 A certain other man] Called Halldórr in *Ólhelg(Leg)* ch. 101, where the date is given as a fortnight before the earlier of St Óláfr's feast days in the year of Nicholas Breakspear's visit to Norway (i. e. 15 July 1152/53). Snorri also gives his name as Halldórr but gives the date as a fortnight before the later of St Óláfr's feast days (i. e. his Translation, 3 August), giving a date of 20 July.

Slavs] Specifically Wends; cf. *vínðr* in *Hom.* 116.

37/27–34 Cf. *Acta Olavi* II:vii; *Hom.* 116 (vii); *SepÓlhelg* ch. 274; *Mberf(Hkr)* ch. 22. Of the first nine miracles in the *Passio* this is the only one that is not also in *Geisli.*

38/1–39/21 Cf. *Geisli* stt. 58–61; *Acta Olavi* II:viii; *Hom.* 117–18 (viii); AM 325, 36 (1v2–9); *Ólhelg(Leg)* ch. 96; *SepÓlhelg* ch. 278; *HSona(Hkr)* ch. 25.

38/4 two brothers] Storm (1880, 138) attributes the phrase 'Brøðr tveir váro í Vic austr' in *Hom.* (117; 'There were two brothers east in Vík'; followed by *Ólhelg(Leg)* and Snorri) to a misreading of the Latin *duo viri fratres* ('two men [who were] brothers'). Snorri gives the brothers' names as Einarr and Andréás, sons of Guthormr grábarði (*HSona(Hkr)* 334).

38/8 a certain English priest] *Ólhelg(Leg)* and Snorri give his name as Ríkarðr (Richard).

39/21 MS Douai 295 follows this miracle involving the mutilated priest with a miracle story involving an English knight. This additional miracle is also preserved in the Helsinki fragment edited by Malin (1920, 12–14) and in the Rawlinson and Bordesholm manuscripts and later vernacular texts (cf. Introduction p. xxx above). Skard states that this is the story's correct place (1932, 2), although he inserts it later in his own translation (Skard 1970, 53–54), at the point immediately before the Corpus Christi College Oxford text echoes the concluding section of the additional miracle (cf. 54/27 below). This conclusion is otherwise omitted in the Oxford manuscript, although it appears in translation at the end of the miracle collection in *Hom.* (but without the miracle involving the English knight which it follows in the Douai and Helsinki manuscripts). This additional miracle story tells of a knight (*miles*) from Britain who kills his brother and mother in a fight over an inheritance, repents and then goes to the shrine of St Óláfr where he is miraculously relieved of iron fetters with which he had bound himself as a penance.

39/22–40/13 Cf. *Acta Olavi* II:ix; *Hom.* 118–19 (ix); *Ólhelg(Leg)* ch. 97; *SepÓlhelg* ch. 186; *Ólhelg(Hkr)* ch. 190. As the author admits, this story is obviously out of place in a collection of posthumous miracles, although it appears here in all versions except Snorri's; he places it during the period of Óláfr's exile in Russia.

39/24 Let us proceed] This phrase marks the end of the material which *Passio Olavi* shares with *Geisli*; from this point there are only minimal differences between the text of the *Passio* and the translation in *Hom.*

39/31–2 the Lord's Day] Cf. Exodus 20: 8–11; Deuteronomy 5: 12–15.

40/9–10 Thus was . . . in Babylon] For the story of the three young men who remained unharmed when burned in a fiery furnace by Nebuchadnezzar of Babylon see Daniel 3.

40/14–41/25 Cf. *Acta Olavi* II:x; *Hom.* 119–20 (x); *Ólhelg(Leg)* ch. 97.

40/30–31 Their iniquity . . . gross heart] Cf. Psalm 118 (119): 70.

40/33 A true lawgiver] On Óláfr as a lawgiver see note to 29/7 above.

41/10–11 rooted . . . precipice] *alte fixa manebat.* Cf. *Aeneid* ii:650.

41/24 the archbishop] This reference necessarily dates the occurrence of this miracle to after the establishment of the archiepiscopal see at Niðaróss in 1152/53.

41/26–42/6 Cf. *Acta Olavi* II:xi; *Hom.* 120 (xi); *Ólhelg(Leg)* ch. 98; *SepÓlhelg* ch. 273; *Mberf(Hkr)* ch. 21. This is the first of several miracles in the collection in which Óláfr saves buildings from destruction by fire.

41/28–29 the city] I. e. Niðaróss.

42/7–45/19 Cf. *Hom.* 120–23 (xii); *Ólhelg(Leg)* chs 98–99; *SepÓlhelg* ch. 275; *Msona(Hkr)* ch. 31. This and the following miracle are absent from *Acta Olavi*; Storm left blank spaces for them in his edition as they are found in the vernacular translation of *Acta Olavi* in *Hom.*

44/17 the dogs' sense of smell] cf. *Aeneid* iv:132.

45/20–47/2 Cf. *Hom.* 123–24 (xiii); *Ólhelg(Leg)* ch. 100.

46/4 nearly every month] Contrast 'every month without exception', line 29 below.

46/17–18 This kind . . . and fasting] Matthew 17: 20 (17: 21).

47/3–17 Cf. *Acta Olavi* II:xiv; *Hom.* 124 (xiv); *Ólhelg(Leg)* ch. 101.

47/8–9 a certain priest of the Roman dispensation] I. e. not Eastern Orthodox. The Latin reads: *quendam latinum sacerdotem*; *Hom.* renders this 'clærcs æins ok kenni-mannz' ('a cleric and a learned man'). The priest was presumably attached to the church of St Óláfr in the city (cf. 52/4).

47/18–31 Cf. *Hom.* 124–25 (xv); *Ólhelg(Leg)* ch. 102. This and the following two miracles are absent from the *Acta Olavi*; Storm left blank spaces for them.

47/32–48/16 Cf. *Hom.* 125 (xvi); *Ólhelg(Leg)* ch. 102.

48/17–50/26 Cf. *Hom.* 125–27 (xvii); AM 325 (2r–v); *Ólhelg(Leg)* chs 103–04.

48/24–49/4 what the Enemy . . . spirit of pride] This passage alludes to the temptation and fall of Adam and Eve in the Garden of Eden (Genesis 3).

49/11–12 freedom . . . God] Romans 8: 21.

49/20–21 the Lord . . . of all] 1 Timothy 2: 4.

49/21 pitied . . . sheep] Cf. Matthew 18: 12.

50/10–12 Truly he had need . . . held him fast] Cf. Psalm 39: 3 (40: 2); 68: 3 (69: 2).

50/27–51/22 Cf. *Acta Olavi* II:xviii; *Hom.* 127–28 (xviii; the text is supplied from *Ólhelg(Leg)* as this and the next one and a half miracles are missing from the manuscript owing to the loss of a leaf; see *Hom.* 127 n. 2); *Ólhelg(Leg)* ch. 105; *SepÓlhelg* ch. 271; *Ólkyrr(Hkr)* ch. 6.

50/29 the year] I. e. 1152/53. Snorri's account has these miracles occur on the first anniversary of the consecration of Christ Church (i. e. St Óláfr's feast day 1077).

50/31 pallium] A 'circular band of white woollen material with two hanging strips and marked with six dark purple crosses which is worn on the shoulders by the Pope and granted by him to archbishops' as a symbol of their authority (*ODCC* 1211, *s. v.* 'Pallium').

51/23–52/14 Cf. *Acta Olavi* II:xix; *Hom.* 128 (xix; supplied from *Ólhelg(Leg)* ch. 106).

51/24 Varangian] The Varangians were a group of Scandinavian mercenaries in the service of the Byzantine emperor (see Pritsak in *MSE* 688–89; Blöndal/Benedikz 1978). The *Ólhelg(Leg)* version of this miracle seems to take Varangian as equivalent to 'Norwegian' ('Þess gato þo marger menn, at hann minndi norrœn vera, firir þui at hann gerðe vapn þau iamnan oc bio, er Væringiar æinir nyta' (*Ólhelg(Leg)* 234); 'By this many people guessed that he was a Norwegian, because he made and prepared those weapons which only the Varangians use'). Skard (1970, 49) translates 'ein mann frå Norderlanda' and notes (1970, 86) that some Scandinavians went to Byzantium as merchants, others to join the emperor's guard.

52/2–4 Now this woman . . . at all hours] Cf. Luke 2: 37.

52/15–53/5 Cf. *Acta Olavi* II:xx (Storm's text ends abruptly in the first sentence of this miracle story, as he was unaware of the existence of Corpus Christi College Oxford MS 209; see Introduction pp. xxvi–xxix above); *Hom.* 128–29 (xx; the manuscript lacuna in *Hom.* ends halfway through this miracle, at 129/10); *Ólhelg(Leg)* ch. 107.

52/17–18 the place . . . his blood] I. e. at Stiklarstaðir. A later miracle in the collection also takes place there (72/18–73/8).

52/29–31 the stone . . . his blood] In *Orkneyinga saga* ch. 104 the same is said of the stone on which St Rǫgnvaldr, Earl of Orkney, shed his blood.

53/5 stricken] The miracle collection in *Hom.* ends here. The following miracles are found only in the text of the *Passio Olavi* preserved in Corpus Christi College Oxford MS 209.

53/27 the eighth . . . Epiphany] The feast of the Epiphany, marking the visit of the Magi to the infant Jesus, is on 6 January. Major feasts such as this acquired a secondary celebration eight days later (counting inclusively) on their 'octave'; from the twelfth century the celebrations were observed thoughout the intervening week (cf. *ODCC* 1173, *s. v.* 'Octave').

54/8–24 Compare the additional miracle involving an Englishman in the Douai, Helsinki, Rawlinson and Bordesholm manuscripts and in the fragmentary hybrid version of Snorri's saga of St Óláfr from AM 235 fol. printed in Unger 1877, II 182. Metcalfe (1881, 96 n. 4) draws attention to a similar miracle attributed to St John of Beverley in an Appendix to Ketell's *Miracula sancti Johannis eboracensis episcopi* written *c.*1170–80 (ed. Raine 1879–94, I 308–09) and suggests this story may have been transferred to Óláfr.

54/24 arrived] Skard includes the story of the English knight at this point in his translation (1970, 53–54); see note to 39/21 above.

54/27–32 Henceforth . . . in recent times] Gunnes takes this clear narrative shift to more recent times as indicative of the beginning of a new section added to an earlier version of the work (1973, 3; 11 n. 9). There is an echo here of the concluding section of the miracle collections found in the Douai and Helsinki manuscripts and in *Hom.* (cf. note to 39/21 above).

54/29 listener] This again implies the text is to be read aloud (cf. 32/5).

55/14–17 Moreover . . . received] The first occasion on which the author vouches for the truth of the miracle story on the basis of his own first-hand experience; whether the 'author' here is Eysteinn or an earlier writer whose work he revised depends on the extent of his involvement in the composition of this section of the *miracula* (called B in the Introduction above, pp. xxxvi–xxxvii).

55/29 the construction of his church] Eysteinn began the rebuilding of Niðaróss cathedral on succeeding to the archiepiscopate in 1161 and oversaw the construction of the transept and chapter house (sacristy).

56/6 forty] Latin *essent*. The manuscript copyist appears to have taken XL (= forty) in his exemplar as the contracted form of *essent* or *esset* (cf. Metcalfe 1881, 98 n. 5). Forty marks was the wergild in Norway in the twelfth century.

57/21–22 in a part of Europe beyond the southern mountains] Latin *in prouintia europa trans montes australes*. Metcalfe (1881, 100 n. 1) argues that the context suggests that somewhere in Norway south of Dovrefjell is meant, with 'Europa' perhaps being a scribal mistake for a Norwegian place-name. There seems, however, no compelling reason to discount his alternative suggestion that the 'southern mountains' are the Alps. Skard (1970, 87) draws attention to the possibility of reading *Eyjabu* (i. e. Øyer in Gudbrandsdalen) for *Europa*, so that the waterfall would be Hunderfossen.

58/33–59/1 the frailty . . . many sons] Since this deacon was a monk (59/5) he would have taken a vow of celibacy. This story takes on further significance, however, in the light of Archbishop Eysteinn's promotion of celibacy among the secular clergy as part of the Gregorian reforms.

59/31–60/9 This miracle resembles that involving the two fratricidal and matricidal French brothers, 54/8–24 above.

60/13 Þórðr . . . Norwegian] Latin *nomine Thordus, dictus norwaice inair*. This is strange; 'Þórðr' is as Norse a name as *inair*, i. e. 'Einarr'. Metcalfe suggests that *inair* might be read *mair*, and this taken as a scribal error for the Old Norse nickname *mær*, 'maiden' (1881, 102 n. 3; cf. Skard 1932, 6 n. 1).

61/6 King Eysteinn] Eysteinn Magnússon (r. 1103–23) or Eysteinn Haraldsson (r. 1142–57).

61/12 such a sweet fragrance] A commonplace of medieval hagiography.

61/19 Bishop Eysteinn] Technically, Eysteinn was *archiepiscopus,* not *episcopus,* though in terms of the three major orders of the sacred ministry (deacon, priest, bishop) an archbishop of course remains a bishop. Metcalfe suggests an English scribe may have been unaware of Eysteinn's true title (1881, 104 n. 1).

61/29–30 suffer with those in affliction] Romans 12: 15.

64/6 the feast of Saint Michael] The feast of St Michael the Archangel is on 29 September.

64/23 the feast of the blessed Mary] It is not clear which Marian feast is referred to.

65/34–66/1 coming . . . the right] Skard refers to a pre-Christian folk-belief that the left was the stronger side, replaced by a Christian belief that the right side was stronger (1970, 87).

67/1 Lundr] The see of Niðaróss belonged to the province of Lundr from the establishment of the archiepiscopal see there in 1104 until Niðaróss was itself raised to metropolitan status in 1152/53.

67/18–19 Estonia . . . the faith] The first organised mission to Estonia took place *c.* 1170 under Fulk, who was consecrated Bishop of the Estonians in 1167. A number of raids were subsequently made on the country, culminating in Valdimarr II of Denmark's crusading invasion in 1219 (Rebane 1989; Christiansen 1997, especially pp. 109–13).

68/32–33 Finally . . . the despot] Cf. Luke 11: 22.

69/15–17 tasting . . . hope in him] Cf. Psalm 33: 9 (34: 8).

70/6–7 to become a public spectacle] Cf. 1 Corinthians 4: 9.

70/13 fish . . . was over] The eating of fish was, however, normally permitted during the Lenten fast when the eating of meat was forbidden.

70/34 there is no concord . . . Belial] Cf. 2 Corinthians 6: 15.

72/16 the Holy Annunciation] This feast is observed on 25 March.

72/23 a nearby community . . . monks] This is the earliest known reference to the Cistercian order in Scandinavia; on the Cistercians in Norway see France 1992, 72–98. Of the three certain Cistercian foundations in Norway, the nearest to Stiklarstaðir was Tautra monastery, but this was not founded until 1207. France (1992, 92–98) discusses evidence for a fourth Cistercian monastery, at Munkeby, a short distance from Levanger in northern Þrándheimr (Trøndelag), and argues that this is 'almost certainly' the monastery referred to here (1992, 96).

72/24–25 the church . . . martyrdom] I. e. the church whose building and dedication are referred to in 52/16–21 above.

73/19 the hospital] A hospital near the cathedral is mentioned in a diploma of King Eiríkr Magnússon dated 13 November 1298 (*DN* I 80).

73/20 three men] Óláfr frequently appears as the leader of a group of three saints in iconography, mostly of much later date than the *Passio*; the saints who accompany him are usually the Scandinavian royal martyrs St Knútr Sveinsson of Denmark and St Erik of Sweden, though he also appears with other saints; see Nyberg 1981.

74/25 miracle] There is no *explicit*, and the remainder of this leaf in the manuscript is blank (sixteen lines and the verso).

INDEXES

Modern equivalents of place-names are given in parentheses. Approximate regnal dates are given for historical rulers. See the notes for instances where genealogical information in the texts translated here does not agree with other sources. Since the texts are not consistent in the use of patronymics and nicknames, characters with the same first name are listed here in order of first appearance.

Personal names

Aðils/Aðísl, son of Óttarr 13/18

Ælfgifu, wife of Knútr Sveinsson, mother of Edmund by previous marriage to King Æthelred 25/16

Æthelred, English king (978–1016) 24/4, 24/23

Æthelstan, English king (924–39) 14/27, 15/13

Agnellus, dedicatee of *Historia Norwegiae* (see note) 1/27

Alrekr, son of Dagr 12/30, 12/31

Anbi, voyager to Iceland 10/16

Ásta, daughter of Guðbrandr kúla, wife of Haraldr the Grenlander and mother of St Óláfr; later wife of Sigvarðr Sow and mother of Haraldr harðráði 17/19, 17/22, 17/25

Ástríðr, wife of Tryggvi, mother of Óláfr Tryggvason 17/31, 18/11

Aun, son of Jǫrundr 13/7, 13/10

Belial, ancient Canaanite deity 70/34

Bera, wife of Ingjaldr son of Hǫgni 13/3

Bergljót, daughter of Þórir the silent, mother of Earl Hákon 18/24

Bernard, bishop 25/33

Bjǫrn, son of Haraldr hárfagri 14/29, 17/15

Braut-Ǫnundr, son of Yngvarr 13/24

Ceres, classical goddess 12/24

Dagr, son of Dyggvi 12/27

Devil, the, Enemy (of humankind), Ancient Adversary 48/18, 48/25, 49/1, 49/5, 49/10, 49/13, 49/19, 65/26

Diana, classical goddess 13/20

Dómaldi, son of Vísburr 12/23

Dómarr, son of Dómaldi 12/25

Dyggvi, son of Dómarr 12/26

Edmund [Ironside], English king (1016), son of Æthelred 24/22, 25/9, 25/10, 25/13

Egill Vendilkráki, son of Aun 13/10

Eiríkr, brother of Alrekr 12/31

Eiríkr blóðøx (Bloodaxe), Norwegian king (928–33), son of Haraldr hárfagri 14/26, 15/3, 15/12, 15/14, 15/20, 17/4, 17/34

Eiríkr, son of Earl Hákon, ruler of Norway (999–1015) 21/4, 22/7, 22/23

Erlingr, son of Eiríkr Bloodaxe 15/10, 16/13

Erlingr the Old 17/2

Eysteinn, son of Aðils 13/20

Eysteinn Fart, son of Hálfdan Whiteleg 14/3

Eysteinn, son of Haraldr hárfagri 14/34

Eysteinn, Norwegian king (see note) 61/6

Eysteinn, Bishop, [Eysteinn/Øystein Erlendsson, Archbishop of Niðaróss 1161–88] 61/19, 62/5

Fasti, brother of Óttarr of Denmark 13/17

Fjǫlnir, son of Freyr 12/15

Freyr, son of Njǫrðr 12/13, 12/15

Gamli, son of Eiríkr Bloodaxe 15/9, 16/8

Place-names and names of peoples

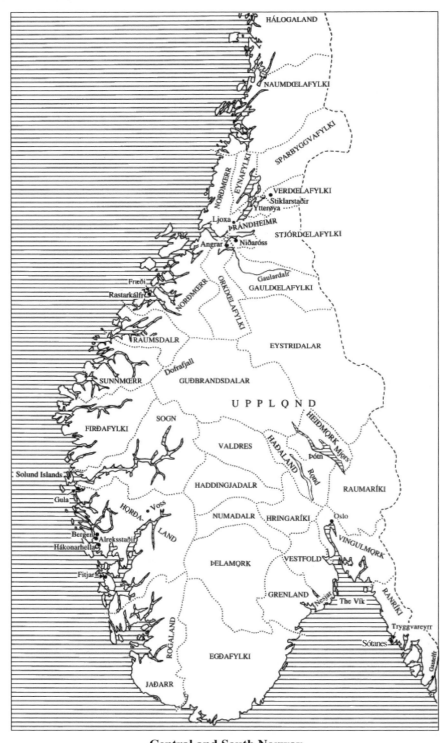

Central and South Norway

Sweden and the Baltic

BIBLIOGRAPHY AND ABBREVIATIONS

Abrams, Lesley. 1995. 'The Anglo-Saxons and the Christianization of Scandinavia', *Anglo-Saxon England* 24, 213–49.

Acta Olavi = *Acta sancti Olavi regis et martyris*, in Storm 1880, 125–44.

Acta sanctorum. Société des Bollandistes. 1643–.

Adam of Bremen: see *Gesta Hamm.*

Ágrip af Noregskonungasǫgum: A Twelfth-Century Synoptic History of the Kings of Norway, ed. and trans. M. J. Driscoll, Viking Society Text Series 10, 1995.

Aigrain, René. 1953. *L'Hagiographie: ses sources, ses méthodes, son histoire.*

AM 325 = Louis-Jensen 1970.

Andersson, Theodore M. 1985. 'Kings' Sagas (*Konungasögur*)', in Clover and Lindow 1985, 197–238.

Andersson, Theodore M., and Kari Ellen Gade, trans. 2000. *Morkinskinna: The Earliest Icelandic Chronicle of the Norwegian Kings (1030–1157)*. Islandica 51.

Anglo-Saxon Chronicle = Charles Plummer and John Earle, eds, *Two of the Saxon Chronicles Parallel* I–II, 1892–99. Reissued with Bibliographical Note by Dorothy Whitelock, 1952.

Bagge, Sverre. 1984. 'Nordic Students at Foreign Universities until 1660', *Scandinavian Journal of History* 9, 1–29.

Bang, A. Chr. 1912. *Den norske kirkes historie.*

Bateley, Janet, ed. 1980. *The Old English Orosius.* Early English Text Society Supplementary Series 6.

Batho, Edith C., and H. Winifred Husbands, eds. 1936–41. *The Chronicles of Scotland Compiled by Hector Boece, Translated into Scots by John Bellenden 1531* I–II.

Beowulf and the Fight at Finnsburg, ed. Fr. Klaeber, 3rd edn, 1950.

Bernström, John. 1957. 'Bäver', in *KLNM* II, cols 490–92.

Beyschlag, Siegfried. 1950. *Konungasögur: Untersuchungen zur Königssaga bis Snorri. Die älteren Übersichtswerke samt Ynglingasaga.* Bibliotheca Arnamagnæana 8.

Bjarni Aðalbjarnarson. 1937. *Om de norske kongers sagaer.* Skrifter utgitt av Det Norske Videnskaps-Akademi i Oslo. II. Hist.-Filos. Klasse., 1936. No. 4.

Bjarni Guðnason. 1977. 'Theodoricus og íslenskir sagnaritarar', in

Einar G. Pétursson and Jónas Kristjánsson, eds, *Sjötíu ritgerðir helgaðar Jakobi Benediktssyni 20 júlí 1977*, I 107–20.

Bjarni Guðnason. 1978. *Fyrsta sagan*. Studia Islandica 37.

Blake, N. F., ed. and trans. 1962. *Jómsvíkinga saga. The Saga of the Jomsvikings*.

Blom, Grethe Authén. 1981. 'St. Olav in norwegischer Geschichte, Königsheiliger in vielen Gestalten', in Svahnström 1981, 27–34.

Blöndal, Sigfús and Benedikt S. Benedikz. 1978. *The Varangians of Byzantium: An Aspect of Byzantine Military History*.

Boyer, Régis. 1981. 'An Attempt to Define the Typology of Medieval Hagiography', in Hans Bekker-Nielsen, Peter Foote, Jørgen Højgaard Jørgensen and Tore Nyberg, eds, *Hagiography and Medieval Literature: A Symposium*, 27–36.

Breviarium Nidrosiense 1519.

Brewer, J. S., James F. Dimock and George F. Warner, eds. 1861–91. *Giraldi Cambrensis Opera* I–VIII. See also Thorpe 1978.

Bugge, Sophus. 1873. 'Bemærkninger om den i Skotland fundne latinske Norges krønike', *Aarbøger for nordisk oldkyndighed og historie*, 1–49.

Bull, Edvard. 1924. Review of Malin 1920 in [Norwegian] *Historisk tidsskrift* 27, 5. række, 5. bind, 310–12.

Butler, H. E., ed. and trans. 1949. *Cronica Jocelini de Brakelonda de rebus gestis Samsonis Abbatis Monasterii Sancti Edmundi/The Chronicle of Jocelin of Brakelond concerning the Acts of Samson Abbot of the Monastery of St. Edmund*.

Bäärnhielm, Göran, trans., and Inger Zachrisson, introduction. 1994. '*De Finnis*, "Om samerna", ur Historia Norvegiæ ca 1190 e. Kr.', *Fornvännen* 89, 161–64.

Campbell, Alistair, ed. 1949. *Encomium Emmae reginae*. Camden Third Series 72.

'Catalogus codicum hagiographicorum latinorum bibliothecae publicae Duacensis'. 1901. *Analecta Bollandia* 20, 361–466.

Chesnutt, Michael. 1985. 'The Dalhousie Manuscript of the *Historia Norvegiae*', *Opuscula* 8, 54–95. Bibliotheca Arnamagnæana 37.

Christiansen, Eric. 1997. *The Northern Crusades*, 2nd edn.

Chronicon Lethrense, ed. M. Cl. Gertz in *Scriptores minores historiæ Danicæ medii ævi*, 1917–18, I 34–53.

Clover, Carol J., and John Lindow, eds. 1985. *Old Norse-Icelandic Literature: A Critical Guide*. Islandica 45.

Cody, E. G., and William Murison, eds. 1888–95. *Jhone Leslie: The Historie of Scotland* I–II, trans. into Scots by James Dalrymple, 1596.

Cormack, Margaret. 1994. *The Saints in Iceland: Their Veneration from the Conversion to 1400*. Subsidia hagiographica 78.

Crawford, Barbara. 1977. 'The Fifteenth-century "Genealogy of the Earls of Orkney" and its Reflection of the Contemporary Political and Cultural Situation in the Earldom', *Mediaeval Scandinavia* 10, 156–78.

Curtius, Ernst Robert. 1953. *European Literature and the Latin Middle Ages,* trans. Willard R. Trask. Bollingen Series 36.

Delehaye, Hippolyte. 1909. *Les Légendes grecques des saints militaires.*

Delehaye, Hippolyte. 1962. *The Legends of the Saints,* trans. Donald Attwater.

Dewick, E. S., and W. H. Frere, eds. 1914–21. *The Leofric Collectar* I–II. Henry Bradshaw Society 45, 56.

DI = Diplomatarium Islandicum 1–, 1857–.

Dickins, Bruce. 1937–45. 'The Cult of S. Olave in the British Isles', *Saga-Book* 12, 53–80.

Dicuil, *Liber de mensura orbis terrae,* ed. and trans. J. J. Tierney with contributions by L. Bieler. Scriptores Latini Hiberniae 6, 1967.

DN = Diplomatarium Norvegicum 1–, 1847–.

Dronke, Ursula, Guðrún P. Helgadóttir, Gerd Wolfgang Weber, and Hans Bekker-Nielsen, eds. 1981. *Speculum Norroenum: Norse Studies in Memory of Gabriel Turville-Petre.*

Egils saga Skalla-Grímssonar, ed. Sigurður Nordal, 1933. ÍF 2.

Eiríks saga rauða in Einar Ól. Sveinsson and Matthías Þórðarson, eds, *Eyrbyggja saga,* 1935, 193–237. ÍF 4.

Ekrem, Inger. 1998a. *Nytt lys over Historia Norwegie. Mot en løsning i debatten om dens alder?*

Ekrem, Inger. 1998b. 'Historia Norwegie og erkebispesetet i Nidaros', *Collegium Medievale* 11, 49–67.

Ekrem, Inger, 2000. 'Om *Passio Olavis* tilblivelse og eventuelle forbindelse med *Historia Norwegie*', in Ekrem *et al.* 2000, 108–56.

Ekrem, Inger, Lars Boje Mortensen and Karen Skovgaard-Petersen, eds, 2000. *Olavslegenden og den latinske historieskrivning i 1100-tallets Norge.*

Ellehøj, Svend. 1965. *Studier over den ældste norrøne historieskrivning.* Bibliotheca Arnamagnæana 26.

Evans, David A. H. 1981. 'King Agni: Myth, History or Legend?' in Dronke *et al.* 1981, 89–105.

Fabricius, Knud. 1917. 'Saxos Valdemarskrønike og hans Danesaga. Med et Tillæg om vore Helgenlevnder og om "Vandresagn"', [Danish] *Historisk tidsskrift*, 8. Række, 6. Bind, 285–386.

Faulkes, Anthony. 1978–79. 'Descent from the gods', *Mediaeval Scandinavia* 11, 92–125.

Faulkes, Anthony. 1993. 'The Sources of Skáldskaparmál: Snorri's Intellectual Background', in Alois Wolf, ed., *Snorri Sturluson. Kolloquium anläßlich der 750. Wiederkehr seines Todestages*, 59–76. ScriptOralia 51.

Fell, Christine E. 1981a. 'Anglo-Saxon saints in Old Norse sources and vice versa', in Hans Bekker-Nielsen, Peter Foote and Olaf Olsen, eds, *Proceedings of the Eighth Viking Congress, Århus 24–31 August 1977*, 95–106.

Fell, Christine. 1981b. '*Víkingarvísur*' in Dronke *et al.* 1981, 106–22.

Finnur Jónsson, 1920–24. *Den oldnorske og oldislandske litteraturs historie* I–III, 2nd edn.

Finnur Jónsson. 1928. 'Ágrip', *Aarbøger for nordisk oldkyndighed og historie*, 261–317.

Flat. = *Flateyjarbók: En samling af norske konge-sagaer med indskudte mindre fortællinger om begivenheder i og udenfor Norge samt annaler* I–III, ed. Guðbrandur Vigfússon and C. R. Unger, 1860–68.

Flom, George T., ed. 1929. *Codex AM 619 quarto: Old Norwegian Book of Homilies*. University of Illinois Studies in Language and Literature 14, No. 4.

Folz, Robert. 1984. *Les Saints rois du moyen âge en occident (VIe–XIIIe siècles)*. Subsidia hagiographica 68.

Fouracre, Paul. 1990. 'Merovingian History and Merovingian Hagiography', *Past and Present* 127, 3–38.

France, James. 1992. *The Cistercians in Scandinavia*.

Fsk = *Fagrskinna* in Bjarni Einarsson, ed., *Ágrip af Nóregskonunga sǫgum. Fagrskinna – Nóregs konunga tal*, 1985, 57–364. ÍF 29.

Geisli = Einarr Skúlason, *Geisli*, in *Skjd.* A I 459–73; B I 427–45.

Geoffrey of Monmouth, *Historia regum Britanniae* = Neil Wright, ed., *The Historia Regum Britannie of Geoffrey of Monmouth* I: *Bern, Burgerbibliothek, MS. 568*, 1985.

Geoffrey of Monmouth, *Vita Merlini* = *Life of Merlin. Geoffrey of Monmouth Vita Merlini*, ed. and trans. Basil Clarke, 1973.

Gerald of Wales, *Descriptio Kambriae,* in Brewer *et al.* 1861–91, VI, 155–227.

Gerald of Wales, *Itinerarium Kambriae,* in Brewer *et al.* 1861–91, VI, 3–152.

Gerald of Wales, *Topographia Hibernica,* in Brewer *et al.* 1861–91, V, 3–204.

Gesta Hamm. = Adam of Bremen, *Gesta hammaburgensis ecclesiae pontificum,* in Werner Trillmich and Rudolf Buchner, eds, *Quellen des 9. und 11. Jahrhunderts zur Geschichte der hamburgischen Kirche und des Reiches.* Ausgewählte Quellen zur deutschen Geschichte des Mittelalters, Freiherr vom Stein-Gedächtnisausgabe 11, 7th edn, 2000, 137–503. See also Tschan 1959.

Gesta Danorum = *Saxonis Gesta Danorum,* ed. J. Olrik and H. Ræder, Vol. I: Textus, 1931.

Gjerløw, Lilli. 1967. 'Olav den hellige. Liturgi', in *KLNM* XII, cols 561–67.

Gjerløw, Lilli, ed. 1968. *Ordo Nidrosiensis ecclesiae.* Libri liturgici provenciae Nidrosiensis medii aevi 2.

Graus, František. 1965. *Volk, Herrscher und Heiliger im Reich der Merowinger: Studien zur Hagiographie der Merowingerzeit.*

Grænlendinga saga in Einar Ól. Sveinsson and Matthías Þórðarson, eds, *Eyrbyggja saga,* 1935, 239–69. ÍF 4.

Guðni Kolbeinsson *et al.,* eds. 1976. *Minjar og menntir: Afmælisrit helgað Kristjáni Eldjárn 6 desember 1976.*

Gunnes, Erik. 1973. 'Om hvordan Passio Olavi ble til', *Maal og minne,* 1–11.

Gunnes, Erik. 1996. *Erkebiskop Øystein: statsmann og kirkebygger.*

Hákherð(Hkr) = *Hákonar saga herðibreiðs* in *Hkr* III 347–72.

Hákonar saga Hákonarsonar etter Sth. 8 fol., AM 325 VIII 4 og AM 304 4°, ed. Marina Mundt, 1977. Norrøne tekster nr. 2.

Hálfdsv(Hkr) = *Hálfdanar saga svarta* in *Hkr* I 84–93.

Hallfreðr Óttarsson, *Óláfsdrápa* (*erfidrápa*) in *Skjd.* A I 159–66, B I 150–57.

Hanssen, Jens Th. 1949. *Omkring Historia Norwegiae.* Avhandlinger utgitt av Det Norske Videnskaps-Akademi i Oslo, II. Hist.-Filos. Klasse, No. 2.

Haskins, Charles Homer. 1927. *The Renaissance of the Twelfth Century.*

Hauksbók udgiven efter de Arnamagnæanske håndskrifter no. 371, 544 og 675, 4° samt forskellige papirhåndskrifter af Det kongelige nordiske oldskriftselskab, ed. Finnur Jónsson and Eiríkur Jónsson, 1892–96.

Heffernan, Thomas J. 1988. *Sacred Biography: Saints and Their Biographers in the Middle Ages.*

Helgi Þorláksson. 1979. 'Hvernig var Snorri í sjón?' in *Snorri: átta alda minning*, 161–81.

Helle, Knut. 1964. *Norge blir en stat 1130–1319.*

Hhárf(Hkr) = *Haralds saga ins hárfagra* in *Hkr* I 94–149.

Hkr = Snorri Sturluson, *Heimskringla* I–III, ed. Bjarni Aðalbjarnarson, 1941–51. ÍF 26–28. See also Hollander 1964.

HN = *Historia Norwegiae.*

Hoffmann, Erich. 1975. *Die heiligen Könige bei den Angelsachsen und den skandinavischen Völkern. Königsheiliger und Königshaus.* Quellen und Forschungen zur Geschichte Schleswig-Holsteins 69.

Hoffmann, Erich. 1990. 'Coronation and Coronation Ordines in Medieval Scandinavia', in János M. Bak, ed., *Coronations: Medieval and Early Modern Monarchic Ritual*, 125–51.

Hoffmann, Erich. 1994. 'Politische Heilige in Skandinavien und die Entwicklung der drei nordischen Reiche und Völker', in Petersohn 1994, 277–324.

Hollander, Lee M., trans. 1964. *Heimskringla: History of the Kings of Norway.*

Hollingsworth, Paul, ed. and trans. 1992. *The Hagiography of Kievan Rus'.*

Holtsmark, Anne. 1956. 'Sankt Olavs liv og mirakler', in *Studier i norrøn diktning*, 15–29.

Hom. = *Gamal norsk homiliebok. Cod. AM. 619, 4to*, ed. Gustav Indrebø, 1931.

Hrólfs saga kraka, ed. Desmond Slay, 1960. Editiones Arnamagnæanæ B 1.

HSig(Hkr) = *Haralds saga Sigurðarsonar* in *Hkr* III 68–202.

Hsona (Hkr) = *Haraldssona saga* in *Hkr* III 303–46.

Hudson, Benjamin T. 1988. 'The Viking and the Irishman', *Medium Ævum* 60, 257–67.

Hægstad, Marius. 1919–20. 'Tillegg. Det norske skriftgrunnlaget i "Historia Norwegiæ"', *Edda: Nordisk tidsskrift for litteraturforskning* 12, 118–21.

ÍF = *Íslenzk fornrit.*

Imago mundi = Honorius Augustodunensis, *De imagine mundi*, in *PL* 172, cols 115–88.

Islandske Annaler indtil 1578, ed. Gustav Storm, 1888.

Íslendingabók. Landnámabók. ed. Jakob Benediktsson, 1968. ÍF 1.

Jakobson, Roman, and Morris Halle. 1956. *Fundamentals of Language.*

Jónas Kristjánsson. 1972. *Um Fóstbræðrasögu.*

Jónas Kristjánsson. 1976. 'The Legendary Saga', in Guðni Kolbeinsson *et al.* eds, 281–93.

Jones, Gwyn. 1984. *A History of the Vikings.* 2nd edition.

Jones, Gwyn. 1986. *The Norse Atlantic Saga.* 2nd edition.

Jørgensen, Jon Gunnar. 2000. '*Passio Olavi* og Snorre', in Ekrem *et al.*, 157–69.

Kemp, Eric Waldram. 1948. *Canonization and Authority in the Western Church.*

Keyser, R., *et al.* eds. 1846–95. *Norges gamle love indtil 1387* I–V.

KLNM = *Kulturhistorisk leksikon for nordisk middelalder fra vikingetid til reformationstid,* 22 vols, 1956–1978.

Knýtlinga saga in Bjarni Guðnason, ed., *Danakonunga sǫgur,* 1982, 91–321. ÍF 35.

Koht, Halvdan. 1919–20. 'Den fyrste norske nasjonalhistoria', *Edda: Nordisk tidsskrift for litteraturforskning* 12, 90–118.

Koht, Halvdan, trans. 1950. *Den eldste Noregs-historie,* 2nd edn. Norrøne bokverk 19.

Konungs skuggsiá, ed. Ludvig Holm-Olsen, 1983, 2nd edn. Norrøne tekste 1.

Krag, Claus. 1991. *Ynglingatal og Ynglingesaga: En studie i historiske kilder.* Studia Humaniora 2.

Kristnisaga, ed. B. Kahle, 1905. Altnordische Saga-Bibliothek 11, 1–57.

Kålund, Kr., ed. 1908. *Alfræði íslenzk: Islandsk encyklopædisk litteratur* I. *Cod. mbr. AM. 194, 8vo.* STUAGNL 37.

Kålund, Kr., ed. 1917–18. *Alfræði íslenzk: Islandsk encyklopædisk litteratur* III. *Landalýsingar m. fl.* STUAGNL 45.

Landnámabók: see *Íslendingabók. Landnámabók.*

Lange, Gudrun. 1989. *Die Anfänge der isländisch-norwegischen Geschichtsschreibung.* Studia Islandica 47.

Lapidge, Michael. 1991. 'The Saintly Life in Anglo-Saxon England', in Malcolm Godden and Michael Lapidge, eds, *The Cambridge Companion to Old English Literature,* 243–63.

Legendary saga = *Ólhelg(Leg)*.

Lehmann, Paul. 1936–37. *Skandinaviens Anteil an der lateinischen Literatur und Wissenschaft des Mittelalters*, Sitzungsberichte der Bauerischen Akademie der Wissenschaften, Philologisch-historische Abteilung, 1. Stück, Jahrgang 1936, Heft 2; 2. Stück, Jahrgang 1937, Heft 7. Reprinted in *Erforschung des Mittelalters* V (1962).

Liestøl, Knut. 1932. 'Når stod slaget på Stiklestad?' *Maal og minne*, 1–28.

Lind, Levi Robert. 1942. 'The Vita Sancti Malchi of Reginald of Canterbury', *Illinois University Studies in Language and Literature* 27, 1–245.

Lodge, David. 1977. *The Modes of Modern Writing: Metaphor, Metonymy, and the Typology of Modern Literature*.

Lodge, David, ed. 1988. *Modern Criticism and Theory: A Reader*.

Louis-Jensen, Jonna. 1970. ' "Syvende og ottende brudstykke". Fragmentet AM 325 IV 4to', in *Opuscula* 4, 31–60. Bibliotheca Arnamagnæana 30.

Lönnroth, Lars. 1963. 'Studier i Olaf Tryggvasons saga', *Samlaren* 84, 54–94.

Lönnroth, Lars. 1965. *European Sources of Icelandic Saga-Writing: An Essay Based on Previous Studies*.

Lönnroth, Lars. 1986. 'Dómaldi's Death and the Myth of Sacral Kingship', in John Lindow, Lars Lönnroth, and Gerd Wolfgang Weber, eds, *Structure and Meaning in Old Norse Literature: New Approaches to Textual Analysis and Literary Criticism*, 73–93.

Magerøy, Hallvard. 1976. 'Ynglingasaga', in *KLNM* 20, 360–62.

Malin, Aarno. 1920. *Zur Überlieferung der lateinischen Olavuslegende*. Annales Academiæ Scientiarum Fennicæ, B 11.

Maurer, Konrad. 1867. *Ueber die Ausdrücke: altnordische, altnorwegische & altislandische Sprache*. Abhandlungen der philosophisch-philologischen Classe der königlich bayerischen Akademie der Wissenschaften, 11. Band, 2. Abteilung, 455–706.

Maurer, Konrad. 1875. *Die Entstehungszeit der älteren Frostuþíngslög*. Abhandlungen der philosophisch-philologischen Classe der königlich bayerischen Akademie der Wissenschaften 13. Band, 3. Abteilung.

Mberf(Hkr) = *Magnúss saga berfœtts* in *Hkr* III 210–37.

McDougall, David and Ian, ed. and trans. 1998. *Theodoricus monachus: An Account of the Ancient History of the Norwegian Kings*. With an Introduction by Peter Foote. Viking Society Text Series 11.

McTurk, R. W. 1974–77. 'Sacral Kingship in Ancient Scandinavia: A Review of Some Recent Writings', *Saga-Book* 19, 139–69.

McTurk, Rory. 1993. 'Kingship', in *MSE* 353–55.

McTurk, Rory. 1994–97. 'Scandinavian Sacral Kingship Revisited', *Saga-Book* 24, 19–32.

Meissner, Rudolf. 1902. *Die Strengleikar: Ein Beitrag zur Geschichte der altnordischen Prosalitteratur.*

Metcalfe, F., ed. 1881. *Passio et miracula beati Olaui.*

Mgóð(Hkr) = *Magnúss saga góða* in *Hkr* III 3–67.

Mortensen, Lars Boje. 2000a. 'Olav den Helliges mirakler i det 12. årh.: streng tekstkontrol eller fri fabuleren?' in Ekrem *et al.* 2000, 89–107.

Mortensen, Lars Boje. 2000b. 'The Anchin Manuscript of *Passio Olaui* (Douai 295), William of Jumièges, and Theodoricus Monachus: New Evidence for Intellectual Relations between Norway and France in the 12th Century', *Symbolae Osloenses* 75, 165–89.

Moseng, Ole Georg. 1992. 'The Dragon in the Hole: The Myths About "Akersberg" and Medieval Mining in Norway', *Collegium Medievale* 5, 45–72.

MSE = Phillip Pulsiano, ed. 1993. *Medieval Scandinavia. An Encyclopedia.*

Msk = *Morkinskinna,* ed. Finnur Jónsson, 1932. STUAGNL 53. See also Andersson and Gade 2000.

Msona(Hkr) = *Magnússona saga* in *Hkr* III 238–77.

Munch, P. A., ed. 1850. *Symbolae ad historiam antiquiorem rerum Norvegicarum.*

Munch, P. A. 1855. *Det norske folks historie* II.

Njáls saga = *Brennu-Njáls saga,* ed. Einar Ól. Sveinsson, 1954. ÍF 12.

Nordal, Sigurður. 1914. *Om Olaf den helliges saga: En kritisk undersøgelse.*

Nóregskonungatal in *Skjd.* A I 579–89, B I 575–90.

'Norwegian Medieval Latin Literature'. 1997. *Symbolae Osloenses: Norwegian Journal of Greek and Latin Studies* 72, 195.

Nyberg, Tore. 1981. 'St. Olav als der Erste einer Dreiergruppe von Heiligen', in Svahnström 1981, 69–84.

ODCC = *The Oxford Dictionary of the Christian Church,* ed. F. L. Cross, 3rd edn, ed. E. A. Livingstone, 1997.

Oddr = *Saga Óláfs Tryggvasonar af Oddr Snorrason munk,* ed. Finnur Jónsson, 1932.

ODS = David Hugh Farmer, *The Oxford Dictionary of Saints,* 4th edn, 1997.

Ólafia Einarsdóttir. 1964. *Studier i kronologisk metode i tidlig islandsk historieskrivning.* Bibliotheca historica Lundensis 13.

Ólafur Halldórsson. 1978. *Grænland í miðaldaritum.*

Oldest saga of St Óláfr see Storm 1893.

Old Norwegian Homily Book = *Hom.*

Ólhelg(Hkr) = Snorri Sturluson, *Óláfs saga helga,* in *Hkr* II.

Ólhelg(Leg) = *Olafs saga hins helga: Die* 'Legendarische Saga' *über Olaf den Heiligen (Hs. Delagard. saml. nr.8^{11}),* ed. and trans. Anne Heinrichs, Doris Jahnsen, Elke Radicke and Hartmut Röhn, 1982.

Ólkyrr(Hkr) = *Óláfs saga kyrra* in *Hkr* III 203–09.

ÓlTrygg(Hkr) = *Óláfs saga Tryggvasonar* in *Hkr* I 225–372.

Orderic Vitalis, *Historia ecclesiastica* = Marjorie Chibnall, ed. and trans., *The Ecclesiastical History of Orderic Vitalis* I–VI, 1969–80.

Orkneyinga saga, ed. Finnbogi Guðmundsson, 1965. ÍF 34.

Óttarr svarti, *Hǫfuðlausn* in *Skjd.* A I 290–96, B I 268–72.

Paasche, Fredrik. 1957. *Norges og Islands litteratur inntil utgangen av middelalderen,* new edn by Anne Holtsmark.

Passio Olavi see Metcalfe 1881.

Petersohn, Jürgen, ed. 1994. *Politik und Heiligenverehrung im Hochmittelalter.* Konstanzer Arbeitskreis für mittelalterliche Geschichte: Vorträge und Forschungen 42.

PL = *Patrologiae cursus completus, Series latina* 1–221, ed. J. P. Migne, 1844–64.

Pliny, *Naturalis historia* = Pline l'ancien, *Histoire naturelle, livre IX,* ed. E. de Saint-Denis, 1955.

Poppe, Andrzej. 1994. 'Politik und Heiligenverehrung in der Kiever Rus': Der apostelgleiche Herrscher und seine Märtyrersöhne', in Petersohn, 403–22.

Raine, James, ed. 1879–94. *The Historians of the Church of York and its Archbishops* I–III, Rolls Series 71.

Rausing, Gad. 1993. 'Ynglinga saga', in *MSE* 739–40.

Rebane, Peter. 1989. 'Denmark, the Papacy and the Christianization of Estonia', in *Gli inizi del cristianesimo in Livonia-Lettonia,* 171–201.

Ridyard, Susan J. 1988. *The Royal Saints of Anglo-Saxon England: A Study of West Saxon and East Anglian Cults.*

Robberstad, Knut. 1949–51. 'Ordet patria i Historia Norvegiæ', [Norwegian] *Historisk tidsskrift* 35, 187–91.

Rollason, D. W. 1983. 'The Cults of Murdered Royal Saints in Anglo-Saxon England', *Anglo-Saxon England* 11, 1–22.

Rollason, David. 1989. *Saints and Relics in Anglo-Saxon England.*

Salvesen, A., trans. 1969. *Norges historie. Theodricus Munk Historien om de gamle norske kongene. Historien om danenes ferd til Jerusalem.*

Sandaaker, Odd. 1985. 'Historia Norvegiæ og Biskop Eirik av Stavanger', *Maal og minne*, 82–86.

Sandaaker, Odd. 1991. 'Mirakelet på Pezina-vollane', *Collegium Medievale* 4, 85–97.

Sawyer, Birgit and Peter. 1992. 'Adam and the Eve of Scandinavian History', in Paul Magdalino, ed., *The Perception of the Past in Twelfth-century Europe*, 37–51.

Schreiner, Johan. 1927. *Saga og oldfunn: studier til Norges eldste historie.* Skrifter utgitt av Den Norske Videnskaps-Akademi i Oslo, II. Hist.-Filos. Klasse, No. 4.

Scott, Sir Walter. [1821] 1996. *The Pirate*, with a foreword by Andrew Wawn.

SepÓlhelg = Snorri Sturluson, *Separate Saga of Óláfr helgi* = Oscar Albert Johnsen and Jón Helgason, eds, *Saga Óláfs konungs hins helga. Den store saga om Olav den hellige efter pergamenthåndskrift i Kungliga biblioteket i Stockholm Nr. 2 4to med varianter fra andre håndskrifter*, 1941.

Sigvatr Þórðarson, *Erfidrápa Óláfs helga* in *Skjd.* A I 257–65, B I 239–45.

Sigvatr Þórðarson, *Víkingarvísur* in *Skjd.* A I 223–28, B I 213–16; also in Fell 1981b.

Skard, Eiliv. 1930. *Målet i Historia Norwegiae.* Skrifter utgitt av Det Norske Videnskaps-Akademi i Oslo II. Hist.-Filos. Klasse, No. 5.

Skard, Eiliv. 1930–33. 'Merknader til Passio Olavi', [Norwegian] *Historisk tidsskrift* 29, 5. række 8. bind, 365–70.

Skard, Eiliv. 1932. *Sprache und Stil der Passio Olavi.* Avhandlinger utgitt av Det Norske Videnskaps-Akademi i Oslo II. Hist.-Filos. Klasse, No. 1.

Skard, Eiliv, trans. 1970. *Passio Olavi: Lidingssoga og under-gjerningane åt den heilage Olav*, 2nd edn. Norrøne bokverk 46.

Skjd. = Finnur Jónsson, ed., *Den norsk-islandske Skjaldedigtning*, A I–II Tekst efter Håndskrifterne; B I–II Rettet Tekst, 1912–15.

Smalley, Beryl. 1974. *Historians in the Middle Ages.*

Snorri Sturluson, *Edda: Prologue and Gylfaginning*, ed. Anthony Faulkes, 1982.

Snorri Sturluson, *Edda: Skáldskaparmál*, ed. Anthony Faulkes, 1998.

Solinus, C. Julius, *Collectanea rerum memorabilium*, ed. Th. Mommsen, 2nd edn, 1958.

Steinnes, Asgaut. 1946–48. 'Ikring Historia Norvegiæ', [Norwegian] *Historisk tidsskrift* 34, 1–61.

Steinnes, Asgaut. 1949–51. 'Meir om Historia Norvegiæ', [Norwegian] *Historisk tidsskrift* 35, 173–87.

Steinnes, Asgaut. 1965. 'Om kjeldene til eit arbeid av Anders Foss om kongsætti i Noreg og sumt om dei eldste Noregs-sogene', *Maal og minne*, 1–44.

Storm, Gustav. 1873. 'Yderligere bemærkninger om den skotske *Historia Norvegiæ*', *Aarbøger for nordisk oldkyndighed og historie*, 361–85.

Storm, Gustav, ed. 1880. *Monumenta historica Norvegiæ.*

Storm, Gustav, ed. 1893. *Otte brudstykker af den ældste saga om Olav den hellige.* Det norske historiske kildeskriftfonds skrifter 29.

Ström, Folke. 1974. *Níð, Ergi and Old Norse Moral Attitudes.*

STUAGNL = Samfund til udgivelse af gammel nordisk litteratur.

Stubbs, William, ed. 1868–71. *Chronica magistri Rogeri de Houedene* I–IV. Rolls Series 51.

Svahnström, Gunnar, ed. 1981. *St. Olav, seine Zeit und sein Kult.* Acta Visbyensia 6.

Sverris saga etter Cod. AM 327 4, ed. Gustav Indrebø, 1920.

Theodoricus monachus, *Historia de antiquitate regum Norwagiensium*, in Storm 1880, 1–68. See also McDougall, David and Ian 1998.

Thorpe, Lewis, trans. 1978. Gerald of Wales, *The Journey Through Wales. The Description of Wales.*

Tolley, Clive. 1994. 'The Shamanic Séance in the *Historia Norvegiae*', *Shaman: Journal of the International Society for Shamanistic Research* 2, 135–56.

Tolley, Clive. 1995. '*Vǫrðr* and *Gandr*: Helping Spirits in Norse Magic', *Arkiv för nordisk filologi* 110, 57–75.

Tolley, Clive. 1996. 'Sources for Snorri's Depiction of Óðinn in *Ynglinga Saga*: Lappish Shamanism and the *Historia Norvegiae*', *Maal og minne*, 67–79.

Tschan, Francis J., trans. 1959. *Adam of Bremen: History of the Archbishops of Hamburg-Bremen.* Records of Civilization Sources and Studies 53.

Turville-Petre, G. 1967. *Origins of Icelandic Literature.*

Ulset, Tor. 1983. *Det genetiske forholdet mellom Ágrip, Historia Norwegiæ og Historia de antiquitate regum Norwagiensium: En analyse med utgangspunkt i oversettelsesteknikk samt en diskusjon omkring begrepet "latinisme" i samband med norrøne tekster.*

Unger, C. R., ed. 1877. *Heilagra manna søgur: Fortællinger og legender om hellige mænd og kvinder* I–II.

van Houts, Elisabeth M. C., ed. and trans. 1992–95. *The Gesta Normannorum Ducum of William of Jumièges, Orderic Vitalis, and Robert of Torigni* I–II.

VSD = M. Cl. Gertz, ed., *Vitae sanctorum Danorum* I–III, 1908–12.

Ward, Benedicta. 1982. *Miracles and the Medieval Mind: Theory, Record and Event 1000–1215.*

Warren, F. E., ed. 1883. *The Leofric Missal.*

Whaley, Diana. 1987. 'The Miracles of S. Olaf in Snorri Sturluson's *Heimskringla*', in James E. Knirk, ed., *Proceedings of the Tenth Viking Congress: Larkollen, Norway, 1985*, 325–42. Universitetets Oldsaksamlings Skrifter, Ny rekke 9.

White, Hayden. 1978. *Tropics of Discourse: Essays in Cultural Criticism.*

William of Jumièges: see van Houts 1992–95.

Yngl. = *Ynglinga saga* in *Hkr* I 9–83.

Ynglingatal in *Skjd.* A I 7–13, B I 7–14.

Qrvar-Odds saga, ed. R. C. Boer. 1888.

Østrem, Eyolf. 2000. 'Om en nyoppdaget Olavslegende', in Ekrem *et al.*, 186–224.